362.838   Silverman
S587h   Helping women cope
                 with grief

Glendale College
Library

**HELPING WOMEN
COPE WITH GRIEF**

DISCARD

SAGE HUMAN SERVICES GUIDES, VOLUME 25

SAGE HUMAN SERVICES GUIDES

a series of books edited by ARMAND LAUFFER and published in cooperation with the Continuing Education Program in the Human Services of the University of Michigan School of Social Work.

A **SAGE** HUMAN SERVICES GUIDE **25**

HELPING WOMEN COPE WITH GRIEF

Phyllis R. SILVERMAN

Published in cooperation with the Continuing Education Program in the Human Services of the University of Michigan School of Social Work

 SAGE PUBLICATIONS   Beverly Hills   London

362.838
S587h

Copyright © 1981 by Sage Publications, Inc.

All rights reserved. No part of this book may be reproduced or utilized in any form or by any means, electronic or mechanical, including photocopying, recording, or by any information storage and retrieval system, without permission in writing from the publisher.

For information address:

SAGE Publications, Inc.
275 South Beverly Drive
Beverly Hills, California 90212

SAGE Publications Ltd
28 Banner Street
London EC1Y 8QE, England

Printed in the United States of America

Library of Congress Cataloging in Publication Data

Silverman, Phyllis R.
  Helping women cope with grief.

  (A Sage human services guide ; v. 25)
  "Published in cooperation with the Continuing Education Program in the Human Services of the University of Michigan School of Social Work."
  Bibliography: p.
  1. Women — Services for — United States. 2. Bereavement — Psychological aspects. 3. Grief. 4. Widows — Services for — United States. 5. Mothers — Services for — United States. 6. Abused wives — Services for — United States. I. Title   II. Series: Sage human services guides ; v. 25.
  HV1445.S53   362.8′38′0973   81-16631
  ISBN 0-8039-1735-X (Pbk.)   AACR2

FIRST PRINTING

3/83

CONTENTS

Acknowledgments

The concept of this book evolved over a period of years while I was working on Contract 278-77-0038 awarded by the National Institute of Mental Health to the American Institutes for Research, Cambridge, Massachusetts, for the provisions of technical assistance to mutual help groups. Included were a group for widows, one for birthmothers, and a third for battered women. It soon became clear that these three groups of women shared many experiences in common. As part of the project, separate self-study guides were prepared for the members of each group, but were never published. Because so much of the experience of these groups is common to them all, it eventually appeared advisable to bring it together in one book.

The pamphlets, then, serve in part as the basis for this book, and in that sense the women who helped write them helped write this book. First, I should like to thank Elizabeth Hormann of Belmont, Massachusetts, who edited the pamphlets and who contributed so much to each of them from her own experiences with mutual help groups. In turn I want to thank Doris Barnard of *People Without Partners*, Waltham, Massachusetts, and Arlene Thompson of the *Needham Widow to Widow* program for reacting to an earlier draft of the chapter on widows; and Lee Campbell, national president of *Concerned United Birthparents*, and the members of the Massachusetts chapter of that organization whose stories are told in the chapter on birthmothers.

The chapter on battered women is based on an earlier draft written by Nancy Johnston of the *Abuse Prevention Commit-*

tee in Framingham, Massachusetts. I should like to thank her and the women in this group who provided a good part of the data. Finally, I should like to thank Trish Cannon of *Help for Abused Women and Children* in Salem, Massachusetts, for the additional assistance she provided.

Beryl M. Safford of Lexington, Massachusetts, deserves a very special word of thanks. To the extent that this book is a coherent and well-written document, it is a testimony to her skill as an editor. She not only edited this book but also helped clarify ideas and provided me with encouragement and stimulation. Words cannot express my gratitude.

Introduction

Women often find themselves in extreme situations which put them under unusual stress and for which their previous experience has not prepared them. Three such situations are described in this book, which I have written as a guide for professionals in social service agencies, mental health clinics, and other human service organizations. It is my hope that a discussion of the issues involved in these situations can help practitioners become more aware of the way in which women experience loss and consequently become better able to offer more relevant help.

The women whose problems I examine are widows, birthmothers, and battered women. By the death of a husband, an untimely pregnancy and subsequent surrender of the baby for adoption, or eruption of domestic violence, these women have all suffered severe losses which produce grief and mourning. Bereavement is a universal experience, of course, but the way it is expressed and the impact it has may be very different for men and for women.

In this book I take a fresh look at the grief of women and suggest that the way they deal with it can be profoundly and constructively affected by the availability of relationships with women who have suffered the same losses. The existence of groups where women can discuss the problems they share can greatly facilitate their development of confidence and competence and their successful adaptation to the altered roles they must assume in their futures.

In recent years the life experience of women in our society has been given serious scrutiny, usually with the goal of ending any inequities in the situations of men and women. The impetus for this continuing examination is coming from women themselves, who are calling for greater public awareness of the aspects of women's lives that appear to foster helplessness and ineffectuality. Moreover, there is now far more open recognition and discussion of issues, such as out-of-wedlock pregnancy and violence against women, which heretofore were not discussed above a whisper and then only in the privacy of the family.

Women are not only identifying their concerns openly today but they are also actively searching for new solutions to age-old problems. These efforts have enormous consequences for professionals in human service organizations. Traditional practice has been increasingly criticized for ignoring or mishandling problems, such as abuse, when women have sought help. By seeking in women's behavior the reasons for domestic violence, for example, or by using such words as "masochistic" or "acting out," practitioners have minimized and denigrated women's very real problems and left them feeling that they have not been helped at all.

Some practitioners still seem to be basing their consultations on outdated, inaccurate, or incomplete theories about the nature of women and the nature of grief. It is not uncommon, for example, for counselors to focus on anger or guilt as the main reasons a widow has more than the usual difficulty adjusting to her husband's death when, in fact, the real problem is that she needs to change her role from that of wife to that of widow. Told that she must deal with anger and guilt rather than with an inevitable role change, the widow may well feel that she has received no constructive help. Birthmothers have also felt let down when agencies have assumed that their problems were fully resolved when their babies were taken away from them and successfully adopted. The help given these women must be changed to reflect a more accurate and complete view of the difficulties these women experience and of the meaning of loss and grief in their lives. Although this book focuses on the situations of only three groups of women, I believe it will help practitioners to respond more effectively to the losses and subsequent grief of other women, whatever the cause.

Although great emphasis is placed in this book on the value of mutual help programs, it is not my intent to imply that mutual help should replace the help furnished by professional agencies. My purpose is to show that no single helping technique can meet all the needs of a troubled person and that, in consequence, even the best services of any one agency are liable to be incomplete. Other helpers, such as those in mutual help groups, can be an invaluable complement to the assistance offered by professional agencies.

The data on widows, birthmothers, and battered women were obtained in interviews with members of mutual help groups. Many of these exist for the widowed and for battered women. They are scattered across the country and are, for the most part, organizationally and administratively separate from one another. The widows quoted here were interviewed in the greater Boston area and in other parts of the country as well. The information on battered women was obtained in interviews with women who belong to a number of independent groups in metropolitan Boston. The birthmothers who were interviewed are members of Concerned United Birthparents, which is the only organization in the country specifically formed to help women and men deal with the experience of surrendering a child for adoption.

Mutual help groups are the vehicles through which these women have found counterparts with whom they can discuss their problems and search for better solutions to them. Sharing is the essential characteristic of the mutual help experience which distinguishes it from other therapeutic exchanges. The helper may not be a "peer" in any other way of the woman she is helping, but she is equally a "survivor" who has coped successfully with the same problem and has acquired a useful expertise based on practical experience rather than special education.

The sort of help available from women who have had the same experiences has always been available on an informal basis. Today, there are growing numbers of organizations for mutual help with all types of problems. The following characteristics can be said to apply to all formally organized mutual help groups:

(1) They develop an organizational structure, with officers, a governing body, and procedures for continuity of the organization.

(2) The members determine all policy and control all resources — they are both the providers and the recipients of the services.

(3) Membership is limited to people who have the particular problems with which the group is concerned.

(4) Helpers are chosen because they have personally successfully overcome or resolved the problem.

(5) There is a specific assistance program which has evolved from the members' experiences in dealing with the shared problem.

It has been gratifying to observe how many professional human service practitioners have recognized that mutual help groups need not be competitors for clients or for resources. The practitioner and the member of a self-help group can be partners in the promotion of women-to-women helping situations. How professionals can develop constructive collaboration with mutual help groups is the subject of another book in this series, *Mutual Help Groups: Organization and Development*.

ORGANIZATION OF THE VOLUME

This book is divided into six chapters. In the first two, we will consider the nature of grief and examine together the experience of bereaved women in the context of new insights into the nature of women and their place in society. The light a "new psychology of women" can throw on the nature of grief and mourning will be discussed. In the next three chapters the ways in which widows, birthmothers, and battered women experience the grief cycle and make the transition to their new lives and identities are discussed. The stages of the transitional process — which here are termed impact, recoil, and accommodation — as they affect each group of women are explored. Finally, experiences are recounted which show how the women have been helped to restructure their lives by their association with other women who have experienced the same losses.

Readers will observe that, in accommodating themselves to their situations and in developing new "identities," these women do not deny their grief or relinquish their pasts but rather alter their relationship to their previous experience. As they develop a new sense of themselves, these women need to remember the past and acknowledge and accept its influence on their futures. They nevertheless are eventually able to achieve a new feeling of competence and of their ability to control their lives.

In the final chapter the findings are summarized and some of their implications for practice are presented. The material should help the human service worker appreciate how women in these and comparable situations can be helped when their grief is understood, their sense of self reinforced, and their establishment of new identities and relationships encouraged. Supplementing professional care with the mutual help experience is recommended.

Questions for readers to ponder are presented at the end of the chapters in the hope that they will promote a better understanding of bereaved women and in turn an enhanced ability to help them. It is usually difficult to read about grief and mourning without turning inward to reflect on our own losses. At least some aspects of the experiences recounted in this book apply to all of us who form attachments to others. If the material strikes a chord in you, please stop and think about your own feelings and behavior and test the ideas presented here against your own experience.

Chapter 1

SPOILED IDENTITIES

Depression is said to be of almost epidemic proportions among women. The commonest causes of female depression seem related to losses women experience and to the way they deal with the accompanying grief. These losses can result from, for example, the end of a marriage either because of a death or a divorce, being forced to give up an important love tie, or if a meaningful figure leaves. On the face of it these experiences often can seem to be very different but all lead to the common experience of grief. This book is concerned with how women react to loss, the way they express their grief, and how they cope with it. Three dissimilar experiences are examined in depth in order to identify issues common to all bereaved women that could account for their high risk.

The three losses with which this book deals are those of widows, of birthmothers, and of battered women. These represent the range of losses women can experience.

On the surface it would appear that the widow whose husband has died, the usually young woman who has had an untimely or unwanted pregnancy and surrendered the child for adoption, and the woman who is abused by her husband or the man with whom she lives are affected by entirely different circumstances. They all, however, have suffered a grave loss — of the husband, the child, or the dream of romantic love and perfect marriage. The reasons for the grief of the widow are clearly apparent. The grief of the birthmother and the battered woman have not generally been so easily recognized or accepted as justified by their experience. The loss of a dream can have as powerful an impact on a woman as the loss of a person and may be more difficult to deal with. Traditionally, help for the bereaved focused on the extreme feelings of pain and anguish that the mourner felt. While the bereaved may talk a good deal about these difficult feelings, it is critical to examine what else happens when the loss takes place. Each loss, in fact, permanently affects a woman's perception of herself; her identity that was made possible because of the now-ended relationship is profoundly altered. Intervention may therefore need to focus on redefining her identity. In addition, appropriate intervention has to consider society's reactions to the bereaved. In the following text the focus is first on the issues created by society's responses and then on the meaning of relationships to a woman's identity.

SOCIETAL REACTIONS/SOCIAL TABOOS

As a result of her loss, each of these women is in a precarious relationship to the larger community to which she relates. Whether passively or actively, these women have all violated social taboos. In this society, people simply are not comfortable with the fact that other people die, that they can be violent, that young people can engage in premarital sexual relationships and make them obvious by becoming pregnant. Each group has been stigmatized by association with these more profane aspects of life. These women's lives have not worked out as either they or society had expected, and they bear not only their own grief but also the onus of society's discomfort or disapproval. As one widow put it:

> My family doesn't want to see me upset. I have to hide my feelings when I see them. My being widowed disturbs other people, too. I've even noticed neighbors avoid me in the supermarket. It's as though being a widow is like having a contagious disease.

As a consequence of their association with death, with sex, or with violence, widows, birthmothers, and battered women are seen by the larger society as people who are damaged in their identities as wife, mother, or lover. A birthmother recalls the period before her baby was born:

I had my act together. I was going to keep my baby. I went to an agency — I didn't know it was an adoption agency — and someone suggested I give my baby up. That I should be considered a candidate for such an unspeakable atrocity made me rethink my value as a potential mother. I found myself drifting away from my first plan. If I had done something so evil — getting pregnant — they were right and I couldn't be a proper mother.

The fact that these women are usually the victims rather than the perpetrators of their problems somehow does not absolve them of all blame or even responsibility in the eyes of their society. A battered woman remembered her first attempt to get help:

The psychiatrist where my husband was hospitalized kept looking at me. He said my husband was not crazy, and he started asking me what I was doing that made my husband get violent. He made me feel as though I was to blame for the beatings I was getting.

Society would prefer to ignore the experiences of these women. And, to compound the problems caused by society's definition of them, many begin to accept society's view of them as damaged, as somehow "spoiled" (Goffman, 1963). Until recently, women have acquiesced in this general attitude, suffering in silence and turning their feelings inward on themselves. The widow, for example, who cannot go along with society's reluctance to acknowledge her grief and loss and who continues to show it, begins to wonder not what is wrong with society but what is wrong with her.

I try not to cry or show my sadness. I keep wondering why I feel this way when everyone says I should be over it. After all, he has been dead for six months. I keep wondering what I am doing wrong. What is wrong with me that I am not feeling better.

Instead of blaming society for denying her the right to mourn openly, she begins to blame herself for not being able to behave the way those around her would prefer.

Women who have had untimely, unanticipated pregnancies have also been denied adequate opportunity to grieve. They have rather been expected to fold their tents and slip silently away into the night, grateful that other people would give their babies the good, "decent" homes which they themselves could not provide. Moreover, they were advised to forget that the births had ever occurred and to keep their secret from everyone. Adoption procedures were specifically designed to protect both the baby and the mother from any revelation of that secret. Most birthmothers obediently complied.

> I took the advice literally. I forgot. In order to go forward, I never looked back. I pushed the memories down. I repressed the pain. It took a lot of energy, and I used mine for that end. I was so successful that I began to feel that I had never been pregnant, as if it had happened to someone else who may once have inhabited my body. I was always afraid of being contaminated by that other person. In my new life I was very conforming and did very well. No one, not even I, would have guessed what was hidden underneath.

In summary, widows, battered women, and birthmothers have in common that society does not legitimate their feelings and experience, and they accept society's definition of them as damaged. In addition, they have all suffered fundamental and irrevocable damage to their identities as wife, lover, or mother. As a result of their loss they can no longer fill these roles. How much of their sense of self is involved in these roles? Do attachments and affiliations have different meaning for women so that when faced with a loss there are different consequences for them than for men? The evidence seems to indicate that for women their very sense of self is tied up with their attachments and affiliations. Loss can be perceived not as a disruption but as a total dismemberment of self (Miller, 1976). Scarf (1980), in her report on depressed women, found that depression in women happens in one context for the most part: the loss of emotional relatedness. For men, she reported, depressive themes more likely have to do with work issues, status and success difficulties, and with making it in the outer world. It becomes critical, then, to understand the meaning of relationships to the lives of women.

THE IMPORTANCE OF RELATIONSHIPS

Traditionally, women have been raised to accept the values and attitudes of those around them. They have been socialized to be sweet, passive, and dependent — to accept a social definition of their true vocation as being that of wife and mother, dependents in a male-centered world. Their very identities and not merely their status were determined not by their own characteristics but by those of the men they married. Women who did not marry, for whatever reason, were generally regarded as failures and, at best, as pitiable. Valued by society not so much for themselves as for their relationships with others, impoverished women, for example, have used marriage as a way of trying to improve their status (Rubin, 1976). And, in some subcultures, bearing a child, regardless of the mother's marital status, improved her position (Rainwater, 1966). Their sense of self was reflected in their relationships with others. When these relationships were threatened, so was their sense of identity.

Until recently, the prevailing view of the psychology of women suggested that women were passive and dependent while men were active and assertive (Deutsch, 1944). According to this view, an assertive female was suffering from a neurotic denial of her own femininity, a femininity that was achieved only when a woman finally renounced all active goals of her own to identify with and fulfill herself through the activities and goals of her husband and subsequently her children. Whereas men were supposed to undergo an identity crisis when they had to find out who they were vis-à-vis their society (Erikson, 1959), women were thought to be exempt from any comparable crisis because their identitites were shaped by the men they married (Lidz, 1967).

Women had a single option, then — to become wives and, in due course, mothers. Women who found this an inadequate goal, who felt stirrings of independence and assertiveness, generally experienced tensions (Friedan, 1963) and often felt the need to find some unusual circumstance in their lives, such as adoption (Lifton, 1977), to account for the discrepancy between society's accepted goals for all young women and their own interests and ambitions.

Being female, many experts found, meant not having to be a self-sufficient individual (Scarf, 1980). It was held that femininity depended upon relationships, whereas masculinity depended upon separation. Nevertheless, the failure of either men or women to individuate was considered tantamount to a failure to develop. Here was a double-bind indeed. For example, one sign of pathological grief in a widow, it was said, was her "dependent attachment to her spouse" (Parkes, 1972). Yet, if women had been socialized not to develop a sense of self apart from their husbands, what other response could be expected from them?

As recently as 1970 a study was conducted to identify the characteristics of a mentally healthy person (Broverman et al., 1970). Discussing it, Scarf writes:

> Abstract notions of what is "mentally healthy" (as long as sex isn't mentioned) seem to emphasize those "masculine" traits and characteristics (such as assertiveness and autonomy) that are more prized and more valued in our society. The lesser status, less valued "feminine" personality traits — less aggression less dominance, more freedom of emotional expression, more excitability, etc. — were *not* seen as consonant with emotional well-being in the adult individual, sex unspecified. As far as mental health is concerned, the feminine role apparently implies pathology [1980: 361].

Consigned to so dependent a role, it has been quite possible, indeed almost inevitable, for women to view themselves as somehow second-rate, to develop a sense of personal inferiority. Therefore, when their identities were damaged as a result of their experience with widowhood, out-of-wedlock pregnancy, or abuse, they try to live with it. They have, after all, been programmed more or less since birth for helplessness; and society, moreover, has given little validity to their feelings and experience. In the face of events that lead to stress and crisis, they usually turn inward, blaming themselves and feeling guilty. Their resulting feeling of powerlessness is compounded by their lack of self-esteem. When they become angry, as they often do, it is more with themselves than with the external cause of their stress. It is not surprising that depression is now said to be of almost epidemic proportions among women (Guttentag and Salasin, 1976). The combination of stress and powerlessness has been found to be the deadly mix that leads to depression (Guttentag and Salasin, 1976). In the face of society's definition of them as being damaged, which they accepted, women have found that quiet depression is about the least disruptive accommodation they could make to their stress.

THE IMPORTANCE OF RELATIONSHIPS

The new psychology of women that has been developing in recent years has been taking a closer and more objective look at women's actual experience in an effort to separate long-held myths from the reality. Although much of the research was initially directed at proving that there were no innate differences between men and women (Tavis and Offir, 1977), the systematic examination of the ways in which men and women were treated and in turn experienced the world from physiological, psychological, sociological, and anthropological points of view was a critical step toward elimination of the judgmental bias that had heretofore found men's experience inherently "better" or more desirable. Once value judgments are set aside, it becomes possible to study the discrete experience of men and women and to appreciate and acknowledge the real differences that may exist between them.

The meaning of attachment and affiliation to a woman's identity is one focus of these studies. A woman's true identity may well grow out of her involvement with others. Her sense of self may be organized primarily around her ability to make and then to maintain affiliations and relationships. That women do not achieve, or even seek, the total individuation pursued by men could be viewed not as a deficit but rather as a trait to be understood and valued (Miller, 1976).

One observer, studying the behavior of children at play, found that the boys were more concerned with the rules of the game, arguing them out if need be so that play could continue while the girls were more intent on maintaining the relationships among the players than on resolving such differences (Gilligan, 1977). The author concluded:

> The elusive mystery of women's development lies in its recognition of the importance of attachment in the human life cycle. While developmental theorists have emphasized the importance of autonomy, separation and individuation, women have known the importance of others. However, instead of valuing this quality, they feel criticized for weakness [Gilligan, 1979: 445].

How do these insights into the nature of women help us to understand the experience of widows, birthmothers, battered women, and other women who have experienced a loss? If indeed a woman's sense of self is inextricably linked with her attachments and affiliations, it is clearly not possible for her to suffer a loss or rupture in an attachment without feeling that her very identity has been fundamentally damaged. One author comments:

> Important figures leaving or dying; the inability to establish another meaningful bond with a peer-partner; being forced, by a natural transition in life, to relinquish an important love tie; a marriage that is ruptured . . . are among the commonest causes of female depression [Scarf, 1980: 86-87].

When women experienced an irrevocable loss of an attachment — as, for example, to their husbands, their babies, or their romantic dreams — their basic sense of themselves is shattered. They have not only lost a relationship but also a sense of who they are. Unless, or until, they can attain a new sense of themselves and develop new identities, they remain frozen in their outdated selves, grieving, mourning, and depressed. If they are to emerge from these shadows, they must find ways to deal with their loss that acknowledges its permanent impact on their sense of self but that also recognizes the possibility of change, adaptation, and the development of new relationships and other identities. In addition, if relationships with others are indeed central to a woman's sense of well-being, as has been postulated, it may be essential that she develop new relationships before she can fully mourn, which requires her to let go of the past and develop a new self. The nature of mourning, and the ways women can be helped to deal with it, are more fully discussed in the following chapters.

CONSIDERATIONS FOR PRACTICE

This chapter pointed out the importance of relationships to women. Women have generally not appreciated this quality in themselves, but instead accepted society's criticisms which tended to denegrate their need for others. Therefore, when faced with a loss they are doubly bereft. They lose their identity which depended on this relationship and they lose society's support as well. As a practitioner, it is important to understand this meaning of loss for a woman. Of the many losses women can experience, this book focuses on three. Do the ideas presented here apply to other losses you can identify?

The following questions can facilitate your generalizing from what you have read so far to the experience of women you work with, or to your own life experiences. If you make a list of the different losses you observe in women, you can get a sense of the wide range of experiences involved. Can you find evidence of the loss leading to the woman's sense of self being disrupted or spoiled? What roles are intact from which she still derives a sense of well-being? What aspects of her life does this woman value? What does she expect of herself and the roles she plays in her family and in her community? Is there real conflict between her expectations and her current problems that make it difficult for her to act on her own behalf? Is there evidence that these feelings are being reinforced by the reactions of others around her? Is there evidence that her difficulty is being fed by her own perception of her self as ineffectual? Would it be important to clarify with women clients their values about themselves, their feelings, and their rights in relationships?

What help did these women seek from your agency? What help did you offer? Having read the preceding chapter, would you change your reactions or what you offered?

Are there similarities and differences in the way men you know react to a loss and in the way society reacts to them? You might want to answer the questions in the preceding paragraphs replacing the word *women* with that of *men*.

REFERENCES

Boston Women's Book Collective (1976) Our Bodies, Ourselves. New York: Simon and Schuster.

BROVERMAN, I. K., et al. (1970) "Sex role stereotypes and clinical judgements of mental health." Journal of Consulting and Clinical Psychology 34: 1-7

DEUTSCH, H. (1944) The Psychology of Women — Psychoanalytic Interpretation. New York: Grune and Stratton.

ERIKSON, E. (1959) Childhood and Society. New York: W. W. Norton.

FRIEDAN, B. (1963) The Feminine Mystique. New York: W. W. Norton.

GILLIGAN, C. (1979) "Women's place in man's life cycle." Harvard Educational Review 49: 431-446.

GOFFMAN, E. (1963) Stigma. Englewood Cliffs, NJ: Prentice-Hall.

GUTTENTAG, M. and S. SALASIN (1976) "Women, men, and mental health," in L. A. Cater and A. G. Scott (eds.) Women, Men: Changing Roles, Relationships, and Perceptions. New York: Aspen Institute for Humanistic Studies.

LIDZ, T. (1968) The Person: His Development Throughout the Life Cycle. New York: Basic Books.

LIFTON, B. J. (1975) Twice Born. New York: Penguin Books.

MILLER, J. B. (1976) Toward a New Psychology of Women. Boston: Beacon Press.

PARKES, C. M. (1972) Bereavement: Studies of Grief in Adult Life. New York: International Universities Press.

RAINWATER, L. (1966) "Crucible of identity: The Negro lower class family." Daedalus (Winter).

RUBIN, L. (1976) Worlds of Pain. New York: Basic Books.

SCARF, M. (1980) Unfinished Business: Pressure Points in the Lives of Women. New York: Doubleday.

TARVIS, C. and C. OFFIR (1977) The Longest War: Sex Differences in Perspective. New York: Harcourt Brace Jovanovich.

Chapter 2

GRIEF AND GRIEVING

ANOTHER VIEW OF MOURNING

To better understand how women react to losses and to help them reshape their lives in a more positive way, it is essential to first reexamine traditional views of grief. Grief has often been described as an illness from which the mourner eventually recovers (Parkes, 1972). If grief is indeed an illness, the mourner must assume that something is wrong with her as she is assailed by the intense and unfamiliar feelings following her loss and that she can be "cured" of pain and disruption by the right treatment.

For women, the view that grief is a temporary illness is a particularly insidious concept because it reinforces the sense of helplessness which society has traditionally imposed on them. It would be more reasonable to help them appreciate that the pain of grief is a normal reaction to the stress caused by the loss (Lindemann, 1944). The feelings that they experience, even though extreme, are psychologically appropriate and even healthy under the circumstances (Silverman, 1977). It is closer to reality to recognize that the grief-stricken cannot be "cured," but rather are changed by their experience. The change involves giving up their former identity and building a new one.

Mourning is perhaps best understood as a process which starts with a significant loss — whether by death or by deprivation — and which inevitably involves change in an attachment, a relationship, and a self-image. All bereaved women, then, need to learn to accept their feelings, to relinquish the roles they played in the lost relationships, and to create new lives for themselves. They must develop new senses of themselves that are independent of the husband, lover, or baby they have lost. Unfortunately, most women are not prepared for this. They do not know how to create new identities, in large part because, as has been discussed in Chapter 1, they have generally lived restricted lives and have had a limited sense of options available to them. Often they are unaware of the degree to which their identity is invested in the lost relationship and that they need to relinquish this part of their lives and build anew. They do not relate the source of their helplessness and subsequent depression to their now-spoiled identities. Identities are spoiled not only because of society's discomfort with their association with death, violence, or sex. They are also spoiled because the reality of the loss is such that these roles are no longer available to them.

Loss is, of course, an inescapable part of living and varies in intensity depending on what has been lost. Attachments to others are essential for human beings, but cannot remain static over time. Over a lifetime a woman's attachments to her husband and family, for example, are constantly evolving. When she bears a child, although she has added a role to her life, she and her husband have lost some of their freedom. As her children grow, her relationships with them must also change if they are to remain appropriate.

Throughout life, then, there are constant losses — and gains, of course — of varying degrees of severity. Yet people rarely seriously consider just what may be involved in coping with changing relationships and situations throughout the life cycle. Most of us live in the present and give little heed to the future. The book *Passages* (Sheehy, 1976) took the country by storm because it articulated a fact which people are aware of but usually do not acknowledge — that change is constant and

that we often do not know how to deal with it. Whether antici-
pated as part of the life cycle, as death is, or unanticipated, as is
an unplanned pregnancy, such changes can be seen as periods
of critical but normal transition.

BEREAVEMENT AS A TIME OF TRANSITION

A critical transition can be seen generally to have three
main characteristics (Silverman, 1966). Initially, there is an
event or series of events which pose serious problems when a
person's customary ways of coping prove inadequate. If this is
the case, the events may have a disequilibrating effect. A
second characteristic of transition is that it involves a period of
time that can be divided into phases, each with its own proper-
ties. Adaptation takes place as the person deals successively
with the tasks inherent in each phase. Finally, the transition
involves a turning point at which the person must redefine the
role she plays in her social network (Rappaport, 1963). How
they move through these phases of transition is the critical issue
for the women in mourning.

The phases of transition have been called *impact, recoil,*
and *accommodation* (Tyhurst, 1958; Bowlby, 1961). Others
have held that transition involves four or five stages (Kubler-
Ross, 1969; Weiss, 1976). It is the first concept that will be used
in this book. During impact, the person is numb or dazed,
unable to believe what has happened. One researcher attributes
this disbelief to a conservative impulse — not wanting to believe that a change has occurred and that further change is
necessary, the person makes every effort to keep things as they
were (Marris, 1974). The numbness facilitates this effort because it enables the person to continue to perform reflexively in
the accustomed role. A widow, for example, continues to behave as a wife.

The second stage, recoil, is characterized by a growing
recognition of the reality of the change which arises from the
frustration and tension involved in the attempt to continue to
operate as though no change had occurred (Silverman and
Silverman, 1979). According to one commentator, there is a

crisis in meaning, when, because the context in which even ordinary events occur is different, it is no longer possible to live by the old rules, yet no new rules have been formulated (Parkes, 1971). Anxiety is typical of this phase because of the vacuum inherent in being "between roles."

During accommodation, the person finds a new direction and develops a "new" identity. The past is not cut out of the person's life and renounced, but rather the person changes her relationship to it. The gap between the past life and the future life is bridged more easily when elements of the past are incorporated into the present, but with an altered emphasis. Ways have to be found to remember, but less painfully, to provide continuity between the past and the future. The transitional period comes to an end not when a particular event occurs but rather when the questioning and exploring have lost their urgency and the emphasis is given to the development of a new life structure (Levinson et al., 1979).

THE GRIEF OF WIDOWS, BIRTHMOTHERS, AND BATTERED WOMEN

By applying this framework for the mourning process to the extreme situations of the widow, the birthmother, and the battered woman, it may be possible to achieve a better understanding of how all women react to the losses they experience in the life cycle. The view of grief as a transitional process rather than a unified, if temporary, state provides indicators for recognizing how women's needs for relationships affect the way they grieve. Failure to recognize their need to work out new identities and deal with society's assessment of a stigmatized role can keep them locked in the first stages of grief for a lifetime. To let go of their now-outdated role, they need to see that there are other options, that they will not be without an identity if they let go of the past.

How do these women experience the successive phases of transition? Impact, the point at which the critical loss occurs, is easiest to identify for a widow, for it begins with the death of her husband. Sometimes, however, the onset of impact is difficult to pinpoint. Does it begin for the birthmother when she first learns she is pregnant, or when the baby's adoption papers are signed? Does it occur the first time a woman is abused, or when she realizes that her husband is not going to stop abusing her?

In any case, at impact the woman's first feeling is one of numbness. She moves automatically, reflexively, unable to believe, as many widows have said, that this is happening to her. This sort of denial, of refusal to acknowledge the bereavement, serves a useful purpose in that it permits her to continue to function, her previous role definition and relationships still guiding her behavior and protecting her self-image. Birthmothers and battered women are equally disbelieving.

> The first time he hit me was when I was five months pregnant. I could not believe it. A part of me said, "It did not happen." I closed off my feelings and, in looking back, I see that I kept trying to act as if he hadn't done it.

There is no way of predicting how long this first phase of the mourning process will last. Some birthmothers have been known to repress any acknowledgment of their pain for 20 years or more.

If these women were to acknowledge their pain, which is a reflection of the real meaning the loss has for them, they would have to relinquish their images of themselves as wives, lovers, or young women who had never had unplanned pregnancies. They would be, in effect, without any identities at all. Because of the centrality of relationships to a woman's identity, because she so much sees herself in terms of her relationships with others, the refusal to accept such a loss may be more urgent for her than it is for men. This does not mean that the process of transition is different for men than it is for women, but rather that the issues involved in role changes are more central to a woman's very being. As a consequence, women may avoid as long as possible facing the full implications of their losses by trying to carry on as before. The loss may be more disruptive and cause greater stress for them.

In many ways, as has been noted, society conspires with women to reinforce their initial numbness and their reluctance to acknowledge the meaning of their losses. Death, for example, is not an acceptable topic of conversation. Moreover, it is regarded as a failure, an affront which should not have been allowed to happen.

> He had a heart condition. If the doctor knew that people rarely recover from this type of attack, he did not say so. We really believed that he would be cured. We had such faith in what the doctor could do. Then, when he died, the doctor kept saying he was sorry — sort of saying it should not have happened. I would have laughed if I hadn't been so upset. I ended up reassuring the doctor.

Abuse is also regarded as an affront to society. To avoid facing this unpleasant reality, society generally seems to have taken the position that a great many battered women have somehow "deserved" their treatment, that by their conduct they have invited the abuse to which they have been subjected. Many battered women have accepted this judgment and blamed themselves rather than their husbands. They have believed that they deserved to be punished, that they have provoked the abuse, and that, in any case, their husbands were entitled to hit them.

> My mother told me that there was nothing to do but stay. He was my husband. She was implying that he therefore had the right to hit me. She said I must be doing something to deserve this treatment.

> My mother-in-law watched him hit me. I asked her to call the police. She told me to stop crying and to take my medicine.

One woman who was in the hospital for the sixth time because of her injuries said, "Doesn't he have the right to beat me? After all, he is my husband." And if they call the police, battered women are likely to be told just to "kiss and make up."

The more society minimized the plight of battered women and even appeared to condone it by refraining from condemnation of their abusers, the more women's doubts about their own innocence grew. They began to feel guilty and to blame themselves, finding it impossible to challenge or revolt against the treatment they were receiving. They remained numb, frozen in the phase of impact.

The strong condemnation of society for the "wayward" behavior of birthmothers similarly forced them to keep their secret or to face social ostracism. The necessity for secrecy reinforced their sense of guilt and shame and persuaded them that they were in some sense defective. They felt they were stigmatized and deserving of their punishment.

> I resolved to keep the baby. But the agency seemed so knowledgeable that I began to think they were right and I was wrong, and that it was bad to continue on with my plans. I think I slipped into a state of shock. I just went along with their recommendation to show them that I really was a good girl. It meant acting as if I had never had a child.

> When I married we really wanted a child. I was told that I could not conceive because I had endometreosis. I felt that I was being punished for what I had done. I can still feel the shame and guilt, even now, when I talk about it.

All of these women, whether widow, birthmother, or battered wife, have been subjected to a general attitude that calls upon them to repress their feelings and to deny, in effect, the significance of their situations.

> No one else understood what I was feeling, and I was beginning to feel twice bereft — for the loss of my husband and for my friends who did not understand me. It seemed as if the only way to get along was to act as if my husband had never existed. Whenever I mentioned his name, people would change the subject.

The grief of widows is expected and accepted, up to a point at least. The grief that birthmothers and battered women feel has not been recognized generally. Yet it is no less real.

> Since I have never had a part of my body amputated, I can only guess what the adjustment must be like. If I were to lose a leg, I would have to adjust and combat my self-pity. It would be rather hard to keep the amputation a secret — and why do so? There is no shame involved. People would rally to help. But to give up a child is not losing a part of your body — it is losing not only a product of your body but your very essence. I had to keep my secret, even from myself. And no one could respond to help me, to see me as grieving.

> When I realized how bad my marriage was I was over-
> whelmed by a great sadness. I couldn't face what I was losing.
> I always thought I would live happily ever after.

In addition, then, to their serious actual losses of husband,
baby, or dream of romantic love and marriage, these women
experience a more subtle but more corrosive loss when their
self-esteem is damaged by social attitudes that deny the legitimacy of their grief. By withholding from them the right or the
room to grieve, society only adds to their sense of guilt and
worthlessness. Because they are still in the first stage of mourning, these women are unable to evaluate the appropriateness of
other people's expectations of them. They remain numb, iso-
lated, and make every effort not to violate society's taboos by
reminding others or themselves of their very real dilemmas.
Instead they use their energy to repress or deny their feelings.
They cannot yet cope with them effectively and therefore refuse to face the fact that their lives have changed irrevocably. In
the words of one widow:

> Two years after my husband died, I realized that I was keep-
> ing constantly busy to avoid my feelings and to avoid having
> to deal with my grief. I had never stopped being numb.

Inevitably, however, sooner or later, some realization of
their loss comes to women and they begin to feel again. They
can no longer pretend that changes have not affected their lives.
They have reached the recoil phase of mourning.

> It's like you wake up one day and realize you have a child
> somewhere. The realization overwhelmed me. I hurt all over.
> I started to play the radio loudly and was tense with everyone.
> I tried not to think about it, but it didn't work. I had been in a
> deep freeze. Now, I couldn't stop the thaw.

Old habits, responses, and role models are no longer appropriate. These women cannot go back to their former lives, but
they are not yet prepared to create new ones. They look rather
for new ways to cling to the past because their sense of self still
depends on their previous roles, as wife or lover, for example.
They may change their daily routines to conform to their new
lives, but they cannot yet change themselves. They are, in fact,

"between roles." During this phase, all the classic symptoms of grief — the sadness, the pining, the sense of emptiness — are acute. This is a second point at which women can remain fixed in their grief. A chronic sadness will persist that can lead to a depression, to a clinging to the past, if no vision of a more promising and constructive future is available to them.

To achieve an accommodation to her loss, a woman must change her relationship to the past and must develop a new identity for herself. If attachments to others are critical to her sense of self, then she needs a context within which she can form new relationships and see that there are other legitimate roles she can play besides the ones she has lost. She must have the opportunity to form new relationships which honor the legitimacy of her feelings, and she needs to learn new skills with which to negotiate change. She needs to develop a sense of self-sufficiency and competence that she may not have felt before. This new self-confidence will help her to deal with the social ostracism and stigma she may be experienceing and thereby prevent her from developing a lingering spoiled identity.

NEW CONTEXTS

How can women be helped to make the transition that not only changes their relationships to their pasts but also finds them with a new sense of self? Help has to be available not only on the individual level but in the larger context as well. If women are to surmount these problems more constructively than has always been the case in the past, then there must be changes in the society around them, both in the way women are viewed and in the social attitudes that ascribe a stigmatized role to bereaved people. In fact, today the climate for women is changed markedly. Women's suffrage, women in the work force and the professions, the increasing frequency of divorce, in general the emancipation of women from the domestic front, are raising insistent questions about the nature and role of women. Within the past several decades particularly, there has been a veritable explosion of interest in the legitimacy — or illegitimacy — of traditional views concerning the true nature and proper function of women. Women are largely creating this new climate as they themselves reject many of the myths of the past and look more honestly and critically at their own lives within the context of the society around them (Boston Women's Book Collective, 1976).

With much of the reticence of the past dissipated by the women's movement, women are more and more able to turn to one another openly and so to discover that their individual feelings and reactions are not wholly exclusive to themselves but are, in part, normal and nearly universal reactions to the ways they have been defined by the society in which they have been raised. As a result of this sharing, they have begun to question the appropriateness of some of their reactions, to feel less trapped by what they — or their mothers — had assumed to be their natural fate, and to find different and possibly better solutions to the problems with which they are faced.

What women have learned from coming together in these ways has had important consequenses for the kind of individual help available to women experiencing a loss. They have created programs, where even a few years ago none existed, which are usually run by women for other women in similar circumstances. From their experiences they found that knowing there are other women "who have walked in their moccasins" allows women to regard their own present suffering as legitimate rather than simply as an outgrowth of their failings.

> I had talked about killing myself and had left home once after he had wounded me badly in the face. But I decided to go back and "take my medicine like a good little girl." One day he had me pinned to the wall and was hitting me and my teen-age son called the police. Something snapped, and I knew I could not go back to that scene again. If I'm going to die, I felt, let it be by my own hand. I'm not going to let him murder me. You know, I still didn't call myself battered. I was out of the home for a few weeks staying at a friend's. I had been reading all about programs for battered women in the newspapers and there was a lot on the radio. It all went by me. I kept saying,

"Who would put up with that?" Suddenly I thought about my situation and said, "Me." That's when I called for help.

Only after they acknowledge that suffering openly can women begin to cope with it. This may take an extraordinary effort as long as they feel that they are the only ones with this problem.

I had never talked with anyone before about being widowed. Who ever heard of being a widow at age 30? I had never heard another widow say how she felt. When I walked into the room and found 50 other women, I couldn't believe it, and at least half of them were near my age. When we broke into small groups, one woman talked about what she was going through and asked, "Has anyone else felt this way?" I felt a sense of relief go through my body. It was a real physical reaction. I realized that I was normal. Other people have the same feelings.

I had lived alone with the pain for four and one-half years. I never knew anyone else could understand what I felt. My friend saw the announcement of this meeting for birthmothers in the newspaper. It is a relief just to be here and find out that there are others like me. I had to psych myself up just to call Ann to find out about the meeting. I might not have come if she had not called back to arrange to give me a ride. It wasn't easy for me to agree to come. But, what a relief to be here and to know that there are others who feel the way I do.

Here is a context in which learning is facilitated. Women who have been through the same experience fully understand the meaning of the loss and what learning is needed to deal with the accompanying changes. Merely by showing that they have coped, that they have been able to accommodate themselves to the drastic changes in their lives, they provide role models that offer the hope for a brighter future.

If we accept that her affiliations with others are important to a woman's sense of self, then it becomes obvious that to deal with a transition, she needs opportunities to make new relationships. It is the character of these new relationships that is critical. New relationships cannot replace the one that has been lost. From these new relationships they need to learn to be involved in a different way. In a new relationship women need to examine some of the components of their earlier dependency on others for a sense of self and learn to depend a bit more on themselves for the core of their identity. In this proces they may develop a greater sense of autonomy as well as come to value mutuality in a relationship. It follows that opportunities to meet others like themselves, in settings where they are not defined as ill or deviant (as might occur in an agency), and that provide these types of affiliations would be most attractive to them. Women-to-women programs have these qualities. These new mutual help programs are often alternate efforts to those of the formal human service system. Sometimes these programs develop in response to professional neglect of the issue with which they are concerned, as occurred with battered women. Other times, programs develop because people realize they have something to offer each other. In contrast to the professional system which values objectivity and training for helpers in the system, these programs value the personal experience of successful coping with the particular loss to prepare helpers (Silverman, 1980). If these programs do indeed offer the bereaved woman a unique opportunity to cope effectively, it is critical for professional helpers to understand this phenomenon and to find ways to accommodate their practice to it. How this can be done is discussed at greater length in the final chapter of this book.

The following three chapters will be devoted to the process of transition as it is experienced by widows, birthmothers, and battered women. The ways in which association with other women who have had similar histories can facilitate the necessary change and growth will also be discussed.

CONSIDERATIONS FOR PRACTICE

In this chapter the process of grief has been described as a transition. Over time bereaved women have to learn that it is possible to change their relationship to the past, to give up the roles that were related to now-ended relationships, and to build new identities for themselves. The chapter ended with the suggestion that another woman who has been through the experience may be the most effective teacher. Both the concept of transition and that of mutual help have important implications for practice. Consider the following questions to help you in your thinking.

Take a loss from the list you made earlier and see if you can identify how the woman would deal with this loss as a transition. Can you identify how her needs differ at each stage of the transition? How does this analysis differ from the one you might ordinarily make of a client's difficulty? Does looking at the loss as a transition, and identifying the process involved, alter your intervention strategy? At this point can you distinguish between help you can offer and the help offered by someone who has experienced the problem? How can these two types of assistance be coordinated? Do you feel uncomfortable about the observation that a woman-to-woman experience has special value? How would this change your practice?

Women's problems are in part created by social attitudes in the larger community around them. Have you considered how agencies can be involved in changing these attitudes? On the other side, have you considered how much agency practice is influenced by these same attitudes? Do you see these attitudes reflected in your agency? How would you change them? Looking back to the men whose losses you have noted earlier, can you imagine a situation where a man is so involved in a relationship that his sense of self is defined by it? Would the same analysis apply to him? Would he then need other relationships to facilitate his changing? How would you react to this behavior in a man? Differently than in a woman? Would you find yourself using such catch words as weak or dependent to describe him? Would you treat him the same way as a woman in the same situation?

REFERENCES

BOWLBY, J. (1961) "Processes of mourning." International Journal of Psychoanalysis 42: 317-340.

KUBLER-ROSS, E. (1969) On Death and Dying. New York: Macmillan.

LEVINSON, D. J., et al. (1978) The Seasons of a Man's Life. New York: Ballantine Books.

LINDEMANN, E. (1944) "The symptomatology and management of acute grief." American Journal of Psychiatry 101: 141.

MARRIS, P. (1974) Loss and Change. New York: Pantheon Books.

PARKES, C. M. (1972) Bereavement: Studies of Grief in Adult Life. New York: International Universities Press.

——— (1971) "Psycho-social transition: A field of study." Social Science and Medicine 5: 101-115.

RAPAPORT, R. (1963) "Normal crisis, family structure and mental health." Family Process 11: 68-80.

SHEEHY, G. (1976) Passages. New York: E. P. Dutton.

SILVERMAN, P. R. (1977) "Bereavement as a normal life transition," in E. Pritchard et al. (eds.) Social Work with the Dying Patient and the Family. New York: Columbia University Press.

——— (1966) "Services for the widowed during the period of bereavement," in Social Work in Practice: Proceedings. New York: Columbia University Press.

SILVERMAN, S. M. and P. R. SILVERMAN (1979) "Parent-child communication in widowed families." American Journal of Psychotherapy 33: 428-441.

TYHURST, J. S. (1958) "The role of transitions states — including disasters — in mental illness," in Symposium on Preventive and Social Psychiatry. Washington, DC: Government Printing Office.

WEISS, R. (1976) "Transition states and other stressful situations: Their nature and programs for their management," in G. Caplan and M. Killilea (eds.) Support Systems and Mutual Help. New York: Grune and Stratton.

Chapter 3

THE GRIEF OF THE WIDOW

WHO ARE THE WIDOWED?

In the United States there are approximately 12 million widowed people: 10 million women and 2 million men. Each year approximately 850,000 persons are widowed. Some 8.5 million of the widowed live as heads of households, the overwhelming majority of them — 7 million — being women. More than 2.5 children under the age of 18 live in 1.2 million of these households, most of them — 2.1 million — with their mothers.

The median age for Caucasian widows is 48 years and for black widows is 39 years. Widowhood is clearly not solely a problem of the elderly, as is often thought, and most widows must be prepared to live a long time as single, formerly married adults. The average widow will survive for about 15 years after her husband's death. A 1975 survey showed that 30% of all women between the ages of 40 and 75 whose first marriage ended with their husbands' deaths eventually remarried, the younger women generally in about three years and widows over 30 in about five years. Of the women widowed before they were 30, 93% remarried within six to seven years after their first husbands' deaths.

GROUPS FOR THE WIDOWED

Over the past decade there has been a proliferation of groups for the widowed sponsored by local community centers, churches, women's organizations, councils for the elderly, and human service agencies. Most of these programs are modeled after the original widow-to-widow programs developed by the author and her colleagues at the Laboratory of Community Psychiatry of Harvard Medical School during the years 1966 to 1973 (Silverman et al., 1974). Many of the programs involve outreach, help being offered unsolicited to the newly widowed. Helpers in these programs are recruited from among the women who have themselves been helped (Silverman, 1976, 1980). Usually it is the widowed who have approached the sponsoring agency for help in organizing the program. In addition, on a national level the American Association of Retired Persons sponsors a Widowed Persons Service and gives technical assistance to widowed people who wish to start local chapters.

How, for the widow, does affiliation with a group of other widows affect the way she negotiates her transition from wife to widow?

IMPACT: IT DID NOT REALLY HAPPEN, DID IT?

When told that their husbands are dead, most widows say that a kind of numbness envelops them. They feel a sense of unreality and disbelief and claim their behavior became stiff and robotlike. Although now legally a widow, a woman's new status has no correspondence with her social and emotional acceptance of the role. She still automatically thinks, feels, and acts as a wife, suiting her behavior, as she probably did during her husband's life, to her perception of what would please him. Only with the passage of time can the widow realize that continuing to be a "wife" is dysfunctional in her new situation. Indeed, the need to abandon that role and the degree of her reluctance to do so are critical factors in the way a widow copes with her bereavement. In the earliest stages, however, continuing to play the role of wife provides the widow with guidelines to how she should behave and what is expected of her. Her numbness helps her to perform her role reflexively.

The intensity and duration of the widow's numbness can vary depending on whether her husband died suddenly or after a long illness. When death follows a long illness, there is inevitably a certain sense of relief and the shock is not so profound because death has not come as a surprise. Moreover, since all her social and emotional resources have probably been drained in caring for her husband, she is most likely to be exhausted and to feel in a state of near collapse now that the vigil is ended.

> I came home from the hospital. The children sensed that it was over and my son started crying. For three weeks we had known he could not live. The children and I lay down and for the first time since we knew, we slept through the night.

When the husband's death is sudden and totally unexpected, the widow's shock and numbness are likely to be all-pervasive. She has not had time to say goodbye, to think how things might be once she was alone, to make even the most rudimentary and tentative plans. Moreover, the suddenness of the husband's death strengthens the disbelief that to some extent all widows feel.

> We were on our way out to dinner when I suddenly heard this thump in the hall. When I ran in my husband was on the floor. I don't know who called the fire department but it must have been me. Next thing I knew I was on my way to the hospital and I can't remember what happened next except that I called my parents and suddenly everyone was there.

> I got called to the emergency room of the hospital. They would not tell me what was wrong and when I got there he was dead. All I kept thinking about was that I had not said goodbye. There were so many things I wanted to tell him. Now what was I going to do?

> I wasn't there when he died. I kept thinking he was on vacation. If I could have been there I think it would have helped make it more real. Other widows have told me that they couldn't believe it for months and that even a year later they would forget and think of their husbands as alive.

The rituals and traditions that once guided people at times of bereavement have largely fallen into disuse in our society, and many widows have no idea how to arrange a funeral or even what sort of observance they want to have. Yet it is the last public act a woman performs as her husband's wife. Often the new widow will call upon a member of the family to make all of the arrangements.

> I didn't know what to do. I didn't even know how to get him from the hospital to a funeral home. I remembered that my cousin was a widow and I called her. Fortunately she came right over and took charge. She made a few calls and things started to happen.

When the husband and wife have discussed funeral arrangements before his death, the widow may have fewer decisions to make at a painful time, but may have other difficult problems to face.

> He didn't want a big wake with an open coffin. His mother was very upset but I insisted on honoring his wishes. I didn't think I had the strength to argue. I never stood up to anyone like that before. It was almost as if I were suddenly a different person — a part of me was somehow closed off. But I had to do what he wanted. I was his wife. I owed it to him.

The widow with dependent children has the additional problem of deciding to what extent they should be involved in the final ceremonies. The issues involved in the decision are usually ones for which nothing in her past life has prepared her.

> My son has had a whole discussion at Sunday School about funerals and cemeteries. I couldn't believe it. I hadn't paid any attention. Now he was telling *me* what would happen. He wasn't frightened or anything. He was 14 and was able to explain what was going on to his younger brother. They decided it would be right for them to come to the funeral. I needed them and they wanted to say goodbye to their father.

> I always regretted that I wouldn't let my five-year-old come to the funeral. It wasn't until later that I realized he was more frightened by what he *imagined* went on than he would have been by seeing what actually happened.

The numbness the widow feels at this stage is a valuable asset in that it averts a state of complete collapse. As one widow put it, when recalling the necessary rituals connected with the funeral:

> You have to be out of it a bit, because how else could you go through the motions of selecting burial clothes and even

choosing a coffin. If I hadn't been I could never have stood the pain of the fact that this was for my husband.

Although the numbness may temporarily protect the widow from the most acute anguish, it does not necessarily blind her to other people's reactions. While organizing and participating in the funeral, she may become aware for the first time since her husband's death of others' fear that she may break down and behave irrationally.

The doctor kept insisting that I take a tranquilizer. He said that my family was afraid I'd break down at the funeral. It would have been numbing the already numb. I was so angry that I almost did become irrational at that point. Now I realize that it wasn't really me they were worried about — they just didn't know how they were going to deal with that situation.

Throughout this early period immediately following her husband's death, the widow remains essentially a wife — this role is still the center of her life. To some extent she can continue to play that part as she deals with the many practical things that have to be done in connection with the funeral and settling her husband's estate. Involvement in these tasks can keep a widow so busy that she has little time to think or feel. And, even at this early stage, how well the widow manages these affairs can contribute to her sense of her potential for competence and accomplishment.

Some things that have to be done that are particularly threatening to the widow's precarious equilibrium she may choose to delegate to others, but there are others which only she can handle. She will have to walk alone into an empty bedroom, see around her her husband's belongings, eat alone, and perhaps change the household routines. The older woman without dependent children may be able to postpone her confrontation with these changes for an extended period of time.

I slept on the living room couch and ate at my children's every night. It was almost a year before I came home at suppertime. I collapsed. I couldn't stop crying. I was sure I was going crazy.

The widow with younger children in the home has no choice but to carry on no matter how she feels.

I tried not to cry in front of my children. I wanted things to be as normal as possible for them. Then my little one stopped working at school, and the teacher said he was depressed. The children felt it wasn't right that things should be the same now that their father was dead. They thought I didn't care about him.

The children were frightened about the future. After the funeral when we ate our first meal alone we were all miserable. You could have cut the silence with a knife. No one wanted to sit in my husband's chair. Finally I did. Then I made a list of chores that needed doing. I don't know where I got the strength. Everyone got a job to do. My oldest started to cry and left the table. When he came back we knew we would survive.

RECOIL: I THOUGHT I WAS DOING FINE AND NOW EVERYTHING IS FALLING APART

Sooner or later, of course, the numbness that has to some extent protected the widow since her husband's death starts to wear off. Most widows fight against this because it means they must consciously accept the fact that their husbands are not going to return. In the first months, the full realization of their loss and of the changes in their lives it will inevitably bring about is more than most widows can tolerate.

I got a letter from this widow program but I threw it away. I thought, what an awful thing to call me.

My husband had been dead for six months. I was job hunting. The first time I had to check "widow" on a form I had to hold my hand because it started to shake. Until then I had avoided ever saying that word or even thinking of myself as a widow.

As the numbness and disbelief recede, the widow's normal feelings begin to re-emerge and she may experience fright, despair, hollowness, even anger.

We'd built a good life together. Then it was taken away. I felt so cheated. I kept saying, "Why us?" as if anyone had a good answer.

It is not unusual for the widow to feel as though a part of herself had been amputated and with it her identity. She may experience loss of appetite, sleeplessness, or, conversely, a desire to sleep all of the time. She may find herself impatient and restless, not wanting to be with people but not wanting to be alone either. She may begin to feel increasingly misunderstood and to sense that friends and relatives are growing impatient and increasingly uncomfortable about her continuing grief. Some women feel that if they can simply keep themselves so busy that they grow too tired to do anything except fall into bed, they will be able to keep their feelings at bay and not have to think either about the past or the future. They are only postponing the inevitable.

> I have worked for many years. When my children got older I wanted to get out and meet new people and be busy all the time. When my husband died work became more important. At work I was fine. I had supper at various children's homes and then with friends. One evening I came home early and I got panicky. I started to cry and I couldn't understand what was happening to me.

> You have to go through the stage where you feel that, if you don't have a man to get up for in the morning, what's it for? What am I getting up for? I felt like half a person. At that time my own goals weren't enough. When the kids left I had the same feelings, but it was different. I needed them and they needed me, but not in the same way.

The widow's new life may still feel totally unreal to her because she may still be imagining that her husband has only gone away on a trip. She may hear his footsteps at the door, especially at the hour he would normally return from work. She may sense his presence in a room.

> I used to dream that my husband was coming back. He would appear at the door and I would be surprised and then I would say, "You are not supposed to be here."

> I used to hear his car pull in the driveway. I used to look at drivers of cars that were like his, trying to see if my husband was behind the wheel. I'd go to the mall and look at all the faces going by, looking for him. Every time I went to church I

would feel an incredible sadness, for a long, long time. I would picture his casket in the aisle. My list is endless.

Many widows review the circumstances of their husbands' deaths again and again, wondering whether anything could have been done to prevent them. Anger and remorse are not unusual feelings at this time. The widow may feel angry with her husband for not having taken better care of himself. She may feel guilty that she did not somehow do enough. At some point, however, she will have to accept philosophically that "his time had come," whether her husband was a young man or not.

A hundred times I said to myself, "If only I had insisted that we go to the doctor the week before. If only. . . ." I would drive myself crazy, and anyone else who would listen to me. I kept rewriting the script, but there was no way I could get back the happy ending.

The widow whose marriage has not been totally satisfactory may feel guilty if she is relieved that she no longer has to deal with the unpleasant parts of her life with her husband.

My husband really wasn't a nice man. He was very strict with the children and there was never any laughter in the house. I couldn't have said that a few months ago. When he first died I was lost and very depressed. People were good and rallied around me. I cried a lot. As I felt better something occurred to me when I watched my girls. They seemed more relaxed. We were laughing more. Their friends were coming around more. I got so guilty when I put two and two together. I started to feel guilty and found myself coming down on the kids.

The widow's grown children may pose additional problems for her. Often they become overprotective. Sometimes they may be having trouble coping with their own grief.

My daughter flew in from California. She began to run my life, telling me how I would manage now. The next thing I knew she was talking about picking me up and moving me out there with her. I don't know where I got the energy. I was still in a daze, but I sat her down and I made it very clear to her that I could run my own life. I appreciated that her job was to be helpful. I also understood that she had lost her father, and I thought perhaps she had some crying to do. I was right. It was her way of not facing her own grief. We both had a good cry and then I could talk to her, as a friend, about what I was really going to do now. I did need her advice.

My son worried me. He never talked about his father. He was away at school. He came home and, without saying a word, he took a leave of absence from school and got a job. I was glad to have him around. He did not cry, he did not talk. He just needed to be there. When he decided to go back to school, we were both ready for him to leave. We never really talked about his feelings, but we didn't need to.

The widow has to learn to be patient with herself through these stages of the grieving process. Perhaps the most important first step is to recognize that she will feel miserable for some indeterminate period of time and that she will simply have to endure that misery. Knowing that this is normal and inevitable can be very helpful.

I was so proud of myself. I thought I was doing so well. I thought that I had everything under control. I was starting to look for a job and all of a sudden the bottom fell out. I started to cry when my neighbor called "Good morning" to me. I began yelling at my daughter on the phone when she called. No one had warned me I might start feeling this way. I called the doctor and he offered me a tranquilizer. Then I spoke to another widow. She was great. She said it was normal. Once I appreciated that I was bound to have bad days and even bad weeks, I didn't need the tranquilizers any more.

I thought I was doing fine — that I wasn't going to need any help. But I met this widow, and she tried to warn me that things might get worse before they got better.

Unfortunately, it is often just at this point, when the widow most needs reassurance and support, that she may find herself more and more alone. Friends and relatives, who had observed how well the widow was managing during the first weeks, may assume that she is over the worst of her grief and beginning to recover. In any case, they have their own lives to lead and may even become impatient if the widow's need for their support seems to increase.

> For a while my life was so crowded that I needed a traffic cop. Suddenly I was all alone. I guess I had become the fifth wheel people talk about.

> All our friends were people he worked with. When the connection was lost, I was never invited anywhere.

Even when family and friends remain available and supportive, however, they may not be able to help the new widow if their efforts are directed at helping her to avoid her grief. It is only when the widow can at last acknowledge her pain, her doubts, and her fears — when she no longer feels it necessary to present a false picture of how splendidly she is coping either to herself or to other people — that she can begin to make the necessary transition to the different life she will have to create for herself. In this her major problem may be that she herself may not know just what her needs are. Here perhaps only other widows can realistically help her.

> I didn't think I had a need to talk to anyone, but I found myself asking how her husband died, how she managed her money, how she handled her mother-in-law's feelings. I realized that this was the first time I had met someone who really understood, and I had all kinds of needs that I had been keeping down.

> When I met this other widow I knew she meant it when she said she understood. I can't stand sympathy and that's all anyone was giving me.

> After my husband died my girl friend visited. Her husband had died three years earlier. She looked so good. How did she manage to get where she was? She was talking about her new job and was excited about her son's new job. She was even talking about a vacation she was planning. Could I ever think of a life without my husband? Would I ever smile again? At that time I did not think so.

> It helps to share your grief with other people who have been down the same road. I learned that only someone who has had the experience of becoming a widow can understand what

you are feeling. I would say that it is vitally important to be in contact with another widow or with a mutual help group for the widowed. It was like a lifeline for me.

Talking with other widows can reassure the new widow that she is not going crazy because she sometimes imagines that her husband is just away on a vacation, that she need not feel upset that her husband was so poor a patient because even "ideal" patients die, that it was acceptable to feel a certain relief that a bad marriage had ended, even though in this unwanted way. Moreover, what the new widow does not know, widows of longer standing may be able to teach her.

She pointed out to me that I was clinging to my children because I was afraid to be alone. They really did not need a full-time mother any longer. I needed someone to show me what else I could do. I made friends with a group of widows and they encouraged me to go to school.

I needed to hear about all the options I had. I had never thought of myself doing any of those things — balancing my checkbook, buying a house, negotiating a loan.

Widowhood means that a woman must change her life, must face up to living her life without her husband. It means that she must think of herself in the present and in the foreseeable future in some role other than that of wife. The new widow needs to make new friends and to develop new relationships. She has to have the courage to say:

I realized that I had to accept a new image of myself. My world was different now, and no matter how much I may have wished that I could go backwards, it was not going to happen that way.

To make the transition in her life requires of the widow an act of will. Her decision to take hold of her life can be facilitated by opportunities to observe how other women have success-fully bridged the gap between their past and present lives. Not only do these women provide her with role models but they also give her an opportunity to see herself in a different light and often to appreciate her own strengths.

I looked around and saw people who were worse off than I was — they had no money or no family. One woman I know really died after her husband went. The way I was going that could happen to me. I wasn't sure I wanted that and I began to take stock. I was doing things I had never done before, going to meetings of a widow group, driving people there, finding that people were counting on me, that I was needed. I was the one who was always so helpless, and here I was helping someone else. I never thought I could change like that. I knew then that I had to go on living.

As I think back on belonging to a mutual help group, aside from the information, support, and encouragement that the group provides, there is also another dimension — that is the feeling of not doing so badly. In all of us there is a certain amount of pride and of keeping a "stiff upper lip." In mutual help groups members are allowed to let their feelings go, and at the same time they encounter others who are battling not only the same tremendous loss but perhaps added burdens that we do not have. Something within us makes us reach out to that person and we come away with the feeling that we have given to someone else — and what better feeling is there to have?

ACCOMMODATION: THERE SEEMS TO BE LIGHT AT THE END OF THE TUNNEL

Grief is not a disease of which the widow can be cured. Inevitably she will be changed by it, she will find herself looking at things differently than she had in the past, she may even find herself doing things her husband had not wanted her to do, such as working or traveling alone. At times she will feel optimistic, and then find that she is depressed again.

I very often give the impression that I "have it all together," but really I don't. It is a constant struggle and the only way I get by is one day at a time. In the final analysis, I still have trouble believing that he is gone, but I do know that I can't change what has happened. Life is either lived, half-lived, or shelved. I either have to stagnate or go on. It's my choice. We all have the potential and ability to change. It's my decision. We can win or lose depending on our attitude. To lose means to end up totally alone. To have a "win" attitude means that all sorts of avenues can open up and there will be green lights all the way.

During this stage the widow will discover that she can still laugh, that there are things worth living for, and that she can once again enjoy people and look forward to getting up the next day. Although not happy that her husband is dead, she may find that the sharpness of her pain has been lessened when she thinks about him. She can now view him as part of her past without despairing of her present or her future. She can remember that past and cry without becoming frightened or uncomfortable about it. She no longer worries whether other people are made uneasy by her feelings. She accepts that a part of her will always be sad when she thinks about the past, but that that is right and natural.

Sometimes the widow finds that the happy occasions in her present are the ones that evoke the greatest sadness.

> When my daughter received her "cap" in nursing, it was very exciting for me. There was the pride I felt watching her walk up on the stage, but there was also the shattering sense of loss I experienced not having her father there. He idolized her, and he was not there to share her day, and he doesn't know the fine young man who is her husband.

> They had a ceremony for parents when the boys graduated from Cub Scouts into the Boy Scouts. My son showed off some of the work he had done. His father would have been so proud. I had to work at keeping the tears back. In fact we both cried a little bit and so did his sister. Then I remembered and I told him that his father would have been so pleased. He beamed at that, and it made the evening for him.

The widow does not want to cut herself off from the past even if it were possible to do so. Instead, she needs to find constructive ways to remember. Her memories become important for they are a means of honoring the dead and of building continuity between the past and the future. Some women set up funds in honor of their husbands at their churches, some donate flowers annually on their husbands' birthdays, and some become active in a project or area that was

important to their husbands. Other widows have made scrap-
books showing things that the family did together. Children
often want to have various of their fathers' possessions which
show the sort of man he was.

> I saved my husband's hiking jacket for my son. He is looking
> forward to growing up to wear it and to take long hikes as his
> father did. I gave him a choice when we were sorting out his
> father's things, and this was what he wanted.

The widow also needs to repeople her life — to make new
friends. Often she may find these in a Widow-to-Widow program or in a discussion group for the widowed. She needs
others with whom she can share both the good times and the
bad and with whom she can do things.

> If I've had a good evening, I need to share it. I can't get used
> to coming home to an empty house. I have a friend who is
> divorced and we both agreed we can call one another at any
> hour to talk about what happened that evening.

Work can be helpful to the widow by providing an activity to
keep her occupied, opportunities to demonstrate her growing
command over her own life, and a place to broaden her circle of
friends.

> I was scared to death. Who would hire a 50-year-old woman
> who had not worked in 20 years? Someone suggested the
> telephone company. I took my heart in my hands and I went
> in. They were delighted. They knew I needed the work and
> could be counted on. There is an advantage in being older and
> I found a whole new circle of friends.

> I could hardly get up in the morning. But having a place to go
> to was important, and a reason for getting up. We had just
> begun to consider a family when he got sick, so I had no
> children — no one who needed me, to get me going. At work I
> was lucky. For about four months I produced very little, but
> my boss was patient. She found things for me to do that didn't
> require too much thinking.

> My job was routine and boring. I knew I needed a job where I
> was needed, and where someone was counting on me. I had
> worked with my husband as an editor, but never for money. I
> thought maybe I could do that again, and I decided that a

university might have a place for a mature woman. I was right. I work for the Math Department now. I do some editing, do their correspondence, and I work for a group of people who are friendly, supportive, and who need me.

Although some widows never feel comfortable about entertaining their married friends, others have no difficulty arranging such occasions and enjoy acting as hostess again. In reconstructing their lives, widows need to find appropriate ways to enjoy their friends.

My son was getting married and I had to have a party for the bride's family. I panicked — how could I receive people alone? But I looked at my son and I knew I had to do it. Everyone offered to help. My sister's husband took care of the drinks, my husband's brother made everyone comfortable. Everyone offered to prepare something and helped me serve. It was quite an evening. I didn't even have time to think. I learned from this that if I wanted to have some couples over, I should ask someone who could play host for me, like my sister and her husband. It never occurred to me — until someone told me afterward — how good it made them feel to see me smiling and to be able to help me.

The first time I invited old married friends for the afternoon it was awkward. They had to rush home. Now I have a group of single friends and we take turns at one another's homes and spend the afternoon together. I also enjoy Sunday brunch after church.

Most widows sooner or later will have to learn how to deal with possible dates and to realize that when she goes out with other men she is not being disloyal to her husband. She may want quite different things from male friends at this point in her life than she had wanted when she was younger. She may not be interested, for example, in remarriage but rather simply in enjoying male companionship. Her only experience with dating, however, may have occurred when she was very young, and she will have to recognize her maturity and react appropriately.

On my first date I acted and felt as if I were 16 again. Then I realized that I could not approach men as though I were a teen-ager, which was the only experience I had had with

dating and courtship. I soon realized that I did not need to
consider marriage with every man I met. It was just nice to go
out and have dinner or to dance. I also realized that I could
call the man. I did not have to sit home, like a kid, waiting for
the phone to ring.

I could not violate my moral code, and sex did become an
issue. I realized that I had been married and that sex was part
of my life. I still have those feelings. At first I tried to ignore
them. Then someone told me that I did not have to act on
every feeling I had. It seems so obvious, but I needed to hear
someone else say it. Now at least I can admit my frustration,
but I won't do anything that is against my own values.

For the widow who contemplates remarriage there are additional problems. Many women view remarriage as a way to
overcome their loneliness and solitariness. A marriage that is
viewed as a substitute for the one that is gone may not work.
Sometimes friends or relatives pressure a widow to remarry
when she really does not want to or is not ready for a new
relationship. And sometimes the potential new husband may
not be prepared to accept the independence and autonomy the
widow has acquired since her first husband's death.

I would not let myself sleep with him before we were married.
I wish I had. My feelings were very mixed up. I confused my
attraction to him with love. It was a disaster. I knew it the first
week. It took me months to consider a divorce. I could not
face it, and my religion forbade it, but I finally got out.
Sometimes it is better to be alone and lonely than in a bad
marriage. I had had no idea.

My daughter keeps talking about my getting married again. I
wonder if she is afraid I will be a burden if I grow old alone.
But I'm having a good time. I haven't met anyone I want to
include full time in my life. I like not having to worry about
anyone but me.

He may be coming from a home in which his wife was not
independent, which most likely she was not, and he's dealing
with a whole new ball game. You have to be sure you're both
playing in the same ball park.

If both partners in a new marriage were previously married, children — and sometimes grandchildren — may have to be considered. This can sometimes be a problem.

No doubt, unless you marry for the first time very late in life, there will be children from both sides involved. These children may have a natural resentment. It takes a great deal of hard work on both sides. Make sure that each of you has the inner strength to take on a tremendous project. On the positive side, though, there is something beautiful in sharing your life with someone. It brings new meaning and purpose to your life.

The widow is growing and changing daily and weekly. She is acquiring new competence and pride in her ability to direct her life, run her household alone, perhaps raise children alone, manage a job, make new friends. Although she might never have chosen to give up her role as a wife, she may well be finding pleasure in her new independence. She will have accommodated herself fully to her new role when she no longer lives in the past, when she can accept her loss and occasional sadness, and when she can look forward to the future with confidence, hope, and excitement.

I'm doing things I never thought I could do. I hate being alone but I have good friends and we care about each other. I'm even traveling. I enjoy my work. I never thought I'd hear myself say that I don't mind being single.

CONSIDERATIONS FOR PRACTICE

In the long run the widow has to learn to live as a single formerly married woman. She will learn how to do this, in part, as a result of the relationship she develops with another widow. She learns that she can survive even if she gives up the role of wife. Another widow views as normal her inability to accept the death. She can share her own experience "sensing the

presense" of her deceased husband. She also understands the importance of being able to talk about him.

As a practitioner working with widows you have to
sort out when you can be helpful and when it would be of
value to involve your clients with other widows. What
are the constraints on each type of help? Do they, in
fact, complement each other. Unless you, too, are
widowed, you cannot offer yourself as a role model, nor
can you provide the opportunity to share experience.
But you can listen, and you can provide perspective and
encouragement. To be helpful you have to consider how
you react to a widow's reality. Consider what you would
do if a widow complained to you that even a year later,
she forgets and thinks of her husband as alive. Or, if she
said that she cannot use the word *widow* when she
thinks about herself. What would you do if she said that
she feels that there is no future and she sees no point to
getting up in the morning. Do you find yourself quick to
offer inappropriate reassurances or to define these reactions as symptoms of pathology? Are you apprehensive
that she will express the extreme feelings she describes?
Do you relate to her current reality — can you stand the
pain — or do you find yourself turning to other aspects
of her life? How would your reactions be different now
that you have read this chapter?

REFERENCES

CARTER, H. and P. GLICK (1970) Marriage and Divorce: A Social and Economic
    Study. Cambridge, MA: Harvard University Press.
SILVERMAN, P. R. (1980) Mutual Help Groups: Organization and Development.
    Beverly Hills, CA: Sage.
——— (1976) If You Will Lift the Load I Will Lift It Too: A Guide to Developing
    Widow-to-Widow Programs. New York: Jewish Funeral Directors of America.
———, et al. [eds.] (1974) Helping Each Other in Widowhood. New York: Health
    Sciences.

Chapter 4

THE GRIEF OF THE BIRTHMOTHER

WHO ARE BIRTHMOTHERS?

Because the status of birthmothers was always a secret, there are no accurate statistics on their number in this country. In a study conducted in the early 1960s, a group of researchers in North Carolina used the designation "illegitimate" which was included on the birth certificate to locate unwed mothers. They found that in 1960 the illegitimacy rate in North Carolina was 9% of all live births, but gave no data on the number of these children who were placed for adoption. Until recently, however, about 90% of white women who gave birth out of wedlock gave these babies up for adoption. Today only 10% of white women who conceive and are not married surrender their children. Black women, regardless of their status, have always been more likely to keep their children.

In addition to scrutinizing birth certificates, it is possible to use adoption statistics in the attempt to reach a number for birthmothers. Again, of course, these numbers are not very specific. It is estimated that there are between 5 and 8 million adoptees in the United States today (Van Why, 1977). Of these, approximately 60% have been adopted within their families; the remainder are adopted by an unrelated couple. These numbers suggest that there must be upward of a million women who could be considered to be birthmothers.

Little is known about the personal characteristics of these women. The North Carolina study was designed to determine whether the women included could be distinguished from their peers by courting patterns or other personal characteristics. Contrary to perceptions current at that time, the unwed mothers were neither deviants in their communities nor could they be considered to be adolescents who were "acting out." Half of them were over 21 years old, 70% of them had finished at least high school, and the vast majority of them had been going with their babies' fathers for at least six months. The relationship was approved by their families, and most of the fathers were free to marry the girls if they chose to. Not even the degree of sexual activity could be identified as a characteristic that distinguished these couples from other courting couples.

Something more can be learned about birthmothers from the membership of Concerned United Birthparents (CUB), the organization that provided most of the data on which this chapter is based. Its membership is drawn from all parts of the country and appears to be representative of those women who feel able to declare themselves as birthmothers at this time. A recent survey revealed that CUB members range in age from 18 to 56, with an average age of 32.2 years. Their average age at the time they surrendered their babies was 20, but ranged from 13 to 32. Most finished high school and some went on to college for a year or so. About a fourth of the members completed college and earned advanced degrees. Some 60% of these women are currently married.

CONCERNED UNITED BIRTHPARENTS

The first meeting of birthmothers, which ultimately led to the formation of an organization, took place on Cape Cod in 1976. The women who came to that meeting had learned of one another's existence through the Confidential Chat pages of the *Boston Globe*. Lee Campbell had written to the Chat asking whether other women who had surrendered children for adoption were having feelings similar to those she was experiencing many years after the event. Other women wrote in, and eventually Mrs. Campbell asked the *Globe* to write to these women and invite them to a meeting.

As a result of newspaper publicity and public appearances on national television programs, CUB has been able to recruit members from around the country and has grown into a national organization. It is not designed to help birthparents locate their children, but is rather intended primarily to help both men and women who have surrendered children deal honestly with their feelings and their sorrow and to understand how the experience has affected the rest of their lives. The growing number of organizations for adoptees who are searching for their roots has also given heart to birthmothers who have begun to question the adoption process and to seek legitimation for their sense of loss and grief for the children they surrendered.

The remainder of this chapter is focused on how the birthmother learns to recognize her grief for what it is and to cope with it effectively so that she can develop a new competence in the conduct of her life.

IMPACT: YOU WERE SUPPOSED TO FORGET

For the birthmother, the numbness associated with the early stages of grief has been the recommended permanent way of life from the time she first discovered she was pregnant. Virtually everyone attempts to keep the pregnancy a secret. Her own reaction may be one of disbelief — "this cannot be happening to me." In part because she usually is very young, she does not recognize or is not given the opportunity to recognize the range of feelings she is currently experiencing and may have no premonition of those that can assail her in the future. Burying her emotions as deeply as possible has been not only what was advised but also her only way of surviving and of keeping her "secret."

> No one knew I was pregnant. I carried small. I went away towards the end of the school year and had the baby at the end of the summer. Then I came back to school. Not even my best

friend knew the real reason why I had gone away. For 20 years I looked back on it as a dream.

I buried my feelings during that whole first year. I got a job and within the year married someone else. I never talked about it. I did not tell my husband about the first baby. I remember being depressed, but I never told anyone. I didn't even think about my daughter until I had another child two years later. I remember being very sad about what I had missed — all the firsts, the first step, her first word. I would push it aside and go on. I told myself not to think about the baby because the social worker had said to me, "The baby is going to a fine family. Her needs will be met. You won't need to worry about her." At one point I even blocked out the birthdate and later on got confused about the year she was born.

The social worker told me to forget about the baby — that she looked forward to my getting married and visiting her with the other children I would have. It took me a long time to realize what cruel advice that was, and then I couldn't look at a baby without getting upset.

Although well-meaning if myopic relatives, friends, and even professional counsellors may expect them to, the birth-mothers' pain and sense of deprivation rarely go away. Typically, they must expend a great deal of energy trying to repress them and keep them buried. But suppressing emotions does not destroy them. Rather, they manifest themselves in many ways — guilt, anger, an unconscious fear of sex, tenseness and uneasiness around children, a vague fear of discovery.

They would not even let me into the nursery. I knew I had been wrong. But in my heart I knew that this baby was right. I kept my rage and my sense of loss to myself. I was a good girl and I did as I was told. I kept my secret. Sometimes I wonder if this is why I'm not married yet. This is the first time I realize how angry and hurt I really am.

I suspect that my pregnancy nine years ago affects me today, and my current relationships with men. It precludes any ability I may have to choose *not* to have a family. Yes, I do want that baby. Will I ever be free to choose, truly? I have no

children, family, or husband today, partly because of what
must be wise but overly high standards. Maybe I want a
guarantee that it won't happen again, that I won't be de-
serted. But there are no guarantees in life. Although I don't
remember the circumstances that provoked it, I do remember
my current partner talking back to me in anger, "But I'm not
the one who got you pregnant. I'm not the father of your child.
I'm not leaving you. Why are you angry at *me*?"

Some birthmothers report that they resort to drugs or al-
cohol to hide from their feelings. Some conceive a second
out-of-wedlock child, whom they surrender to adoption as an
effort, they later conclude, to prove to themselves that that was
the only thing they could have done the first time. Others keep
the second child as a way of retaliating against the parents or
boyfriends who insisted that they surrender the first child for
adoption. Still other birthmothers become weepy, restless, anxious, and forgetful. Although not all women who give up a child
punish themselves in subsequent relationships, the pain, secrecy, and guilt involved in their experience can profoundly
affect their future marriages and relationships with children.

Some birthmothers marry quickly and promptly have one or
more children they can keep. They appear to be eager to prove
that they are worthy of being someone's wife, particularly if the
birthfather rejected them when they became pregnant. They
may also be seeking the approval of their parents, if the parents
had expressed disappointment or disgust with their previous
pregnancies. The birthmother may well find, however, that
these steps have not constituted a solution.

I got married and had a son. I didn't think about the baby
then. But my next was a girl like the one I had surrendered. I
couldn't stop thinking about my first baby. My husband didn't
know. I had been told not to tell him because he would not
marry me if he knew. Things started to fall apart between my
husband and me. We did get a divorce. Now, looking back, I
think it was because of my secret that I couldn't share. I was
so preoccupied.

My husband knew about my daughter. He never let me forget
it, especially when we found out that I couldn't conceive

again. He would beat on me, and he knew I'd never leave because I thought I deserved this kind of treatment — not for getting pregnant but for giving up the baby and surrendering her to adoption.

As the birthmother just quoted said, the shame birthmothers feel over having become pregnant in the first place often turns into guilt over their "abandonment" of their babies. They may, as a result, either keep themselves from getting too close to their subsequent children or, equally, overprotect them.

Every time my five-year-old wanted to stay over at a friend's house I panicked. I cried all the way home when we left her at her grandmother's for a night. I kept calling to make sure she was all right. It was not like me. My husband finally spoke up when I would not let her go to my folk's house again. He said that I was afraid that I would lose her, too, as I had lost the first child. I was reliving the scene in the hospital when I went away and left my baby for someone else to care for. Every time I think about it, I get sick. I wouldn't leave my *dog* to strangers — how could I have done that to my *baby*? At least I understand my behavior now and I am more comfortable when my daughter visits. I still get panicky but I have better control. I try not to interfere with her having a good time, and her need to experience being away from home from time to time.

In spite of the price she is paying in other ways, the birthmother often finds it easier to remain at some intermediate point in her grieving process rather than to face her pain fully. Her family and friends may equally want to bury the whole experience and may fail to make any connection between the birthmother's past history and her emotional upsets, aloofness, or inability to cope with normal stresses. Even when they do recognize the connection, they may not want to discuss it, either out of deference to her feelings or in an attempt to protect their own.

My father just pushed it out of his mind. He called me some terrible names and had nothing more to say. Since then I've never been close to him. My mother was more willing to talk about it. She knew how much I hurt. But once she was told that it was best to give up the baby, she would never talk about him. He was her first grandchild and she was very upset. She had no way of expressing her hurt, so we both tried to bury it.

Most birthmothers cannot find the words to express the sort of pain and grief they are feeling. Many wind up in therapy, not because of their surrender of a child to adoption but because of other problems which they usually do not connect with that early pregnancy.

I was in therapy to help deal with my feelings about being single. I had just divorced my husband. It was 25 years after my baby had been born. I said out loud that I had given up my daughter. I couldn't breathe. My therapist had to help me get my breath. It took 10 minutes. I started to cry and all the regret and pain overwhelmed me.

Three years after I surrendered my daughter I was in college. I became dysfunctional. I did not want to study, I did not want to go out. My mother kept saying that something must be wrong. Finally I went to see a psychiatrist and told him — he was the first person I had told. I saw him one day a week for four years. He said that I was living in a fantasy world, that I had not dealt with it. I'm still having trouble. I still feel the pain and the anger, not for getting pregnant but for giving in to the pressure and giving up my child.

About a year ago we went to see a marriage counsellor because we were having a lot of trouble. It was around the date of my child's birth. I always have trouble at that time. I sort of go berserk, feel numb, and am very depressed. Don't look at me cross-eyed — I'll chew off your head at the drop of a hat. I did this for five years. For a month around her birthday I would be a bitch. I would cry, I went up and down. I didn't even know it was happening cyclically until my husband finally identified it. I was shocked when he told me that I do the same thing every year. And to think that you are celebrating the birthday of someone you don't even know is alive or not. The marriage counsellor told me that it is like a death — you have to grieve. I told him that I had never talked about it to anyone, although my husband clearly knew.

Anniversary reactions of this sort are not at all unusual for birthmothers, but often go unrecognized.

> I had given up my child and knew I should suffer. I lost my hair because of nerves, and the doctor put me on tranquilizers. You shouldn't put a depressed birthmother on tranquilizers. I became suicidal. I thought about my child when I woke up the morning of his first birthday. By noon, when I was at my desk in my office I had forgotten, but I found myself shaking all over and no one knew what to do with me. This went on and I saw a psychologist and finally got it out. I was having an anniversary reaction every year, and I hadn't made the connection for eight years.

Some birthmothers may appear to function very well, often for years, and may then, for no apparent reason, find themselves obsessed with the past. Their feelings can be overwhelming, and the pain is particularly terrifying because they are not sure whether it is normal for them to experience it.

> Since I had been told at the time that I would eventually get over it, I could not understand why I was having such difficulties now, 15 years later. I could not get the baby out of my mind, and I decided that I must be neurotic. I felt worse and worse about myself. I was sure that I was really very sick.

> I can't tell you what made me start to think about the baby. I seemed to be falling apart after 13 years. I could not get this baby out of my mind. I did not even know what sex it was. I decided to write the doctor who had arranged the adoption after he delivered the baby and ask if he would at least tell me the sex of the baby, to give me some sense of reality. He is a relative. It took a lot of nerve on my part because all those years I never thought I had the right to ask. About the same time I wrote him he called me to tell me he was not going to be able to protect my privacy for much longer. He told me that I had had a girl and that she was asking her adoptive parents who her real mother was. The adoptive parents had gone to him to see if they could find out. It was an eerie feeling. When I got over the shock of the coincidence, I told him that I had had enough of privacy.

Many birthmothers seem unable to speak fully about their feelings and their sorrow until they find a setting where those feelings can be seen to be legitimate and can be correctly labelled. Unitl recent years this has not been easy for them.

> Birthmothers have no easy way of finding each other. It is hard to believe, given the way we feel inside, but we don't tell anyone. How would other people know we are birthmothers?

> Who ever heard of a reunion at a home for unmarried mothers? We lived together for four to five months, but if we met on the street we would be obliged to look the other way. How could we account for knowing one another?

Today there is much more openness about the problems birthmothers experience and about the complexities of adoption generally. The birthmother can easily encounter articles in newspapers and magazines, hear discussions on radio and television programs, or even discover that she has many fellow sufferers through research programs.

> The thing that really started me going was the ad in the paper for a research project. Dr. Grunebaum was looking for women who had surrendered their children. That was the first time I realized other people had done this. This was several years ago now. I went there to be interviewed. Dr. Grunebaum asked me all kinds of questions that I had never considered. I had never talked about it before. I would occasionally cry, but I wasn't reliving everything at that point. I had a good marriage, other children, and everything was basically all right. Dr. Grunebaum asked me if I would like to belong to a group. I went to the Adoption Liberation Movement Association at his suggestion. I cried all through the meeting. I had never cried so much in my life. That's when the whole thing really hit me.

RECOIL: THAWING OUT AND OWNING UP

"Thawing out" is not an inappropriate term to use to describe the ultimate recognition by birthmothers of their deep-seated grief inasmuch as so many of them describe themselves as having been in a deep freeze, sometimes for years. However effective their defense mechanisms of repression, denial, and even a virtual amnesia have been in the past, they now find themselves totally unable to erase their memories and the wracking emotions those memories evoke.

As their minds are drawn increasingly, for whatever reason, to this stunning event in their pasts, they may realize for the first time that they are grieving and probably have been, unknowingly, for years. Like other bereaved persons, they feel terribly sad because of what they have lost, cheated of the time that they could have spent with the lost one, and yearn to be able to turn the clock back. In addition, however, the birthmother may feel bitterness and rage.

At first the birthmother's rage may be directed primarily at herself — she was the one who got pregnant, after all. Moreover, she will experience deep remorse and guilt because she gave up the baby and abandoned it to an unknown destiny.

> I finally told my son about the daughter I had surrendered. He looked at me and said, "And you can never forgive yourself for giving her up. How could you have done such a thing? You could have made it."

At least a part of the birthmother's bitterness and rage are directed to the world around her — the people who might have prevented or eased the traumatic events with which she has had to live but, who, for one reason or another, "failed" her.

> I was angry at first with myself because I could not get my own act together enough to keep the baby. This had been within my power, I kept telling myself, ignoring the pressure I had been under. I was angry because I still had the pain and the emptiness. Then I got angry because no one had given me any advice about birth control. Now I realize that birth control is no guarantee. People get pregnant anyhow, especially me. I got pregnant again on my wedding night. Once it happens, there are all kinds of angers.

> My mother would not help me when the baby was born. My father would not allow the "little bastard in the house." Now

my mother is sorry. She lost her first grandchild, but I lost my baby. If I had had a little help at the beginning, we would have made it.

My mother forgot all about how she secreted me off to a home. She now says, "Well, it was your choice." I can't point any finger of blame. It wouldn't help, and it was so complicated.

Others beside the birthmother have been part of the conspiracy of silence which has kept her secret hidden over the years. If the birthmother can no longer repress her feelings and begins to express her anger and sorrow, she is opening up not only her own wounds but also those of other people close to her. If she has not told her secret to her present husband, there may also be an element of threat associated with any impulse to air her feelings honestly. Occasionally, however, the birthmother may find a family member who is willing to talk about the past. While this can be an acutely painful experience, it can also be liberating.

My mother kept telling me never to bring it up with my grandmother — it was too upsetting for her. One day when grandmother was visiting us she noticed my tension and preoccupation and asked me about it. I told her it was the anniversary of my daughter's birth. Tears came to her eyes. She said that she always thinks about her, too, and has often wanted to talk with me. My mother forbade her to because the social worker had said it must be my decision. The family had to back off. Grandmother had wanted to keep the baby. We both had a good cry. My five-year-old came in at that point and I had to tell her to reassure her about why we were crying. That was the end of the secrets but not the end of the rage. Why didn't I know about welfare? Why didn't I know how my grandmother felt? I felt so empty and overwhelmed by sadness — but very good, too, that it was finally out in the open.

Once a birthmother begins to speak openly of her feelings, she has taken the critical first step toward her ultimate accommodation to her grief — the acknowledgment that it exists and that she is, and has been, in effect in mourning. She cannot turn back the clock, she cannot undo the pregnancy, she cannot recapture the privilege of nurturing that child. She must learn that she cannot be cured of her feelings and that she will never totally get over them. Rather, she must achieve some perspective on them and recognize their role in her life.

> You do have to grieve, but we can't say that it is a death. If there has been a death, then what happens if the child is resurrected? I knew a birthmother who told her child, who had found her, that it couldn't be her, that she was dead. No, it is not a death. It's an emptiness, as if you had lost a part of yourself. I have suffered the death of a child and I have also surrendered a child. I think that the death is easier than the surrender. At least I can go to the grave and I know that he is gone.

> I'm not sure what "back to normal" means. I will never be the same as I was before my pregnancy. It took me at least a year to begin to grow back some skin over my rawness, my sensitivity. One of the things that a birthmother has to learn is to live with the pain, but you have to know what that pain is from.

> When I finally had done all the things I should do — finished college, gotten married, had children — I was still hurting. Then I had to face the possibility that it was never going to get better.

Although everyone who has a serious problem generally finds that only another person with the same problem truly understands all its complexities, getting together with other women who have had the same experience is particularly important to the birthmother because of the secrecy, shame, and guilt that have characterized out-of-wedlock births.

> I wouldn't have known how to talk about my feelings if I hadn't talked to another birthmother. I was like a bull in a china shop. I needed to learn to let things out slowly and to be constructive.

The availability of a group such as Concerned United Birthparents can be of critical importance in offering the opportunity for birthmothers to explore, identify, and acknowledge feelings they have suppressed. Without such an understanding and sympathetic forum, many birthmothers would remain in hiding, postponing or even indefinitely deferring their accommodation to their grief.

> The first thing I would tell someone about being a birthmother is that you have to talk about it.

> You have to acknowledge that it happened, that you are a birthmother — just as you admit to the color of your eyes, etc. You have to say that it happened.

Some birthmothers find that simply sharing their feelings with their counterparts is an adequate start toward the resolution of their pain. They may participate in CUB, but otherwise maintain their secret. Others choose to be completely open about their pasts or may be forced by circumstances to become so.

> My husband always knew about the daughter I had surrendered, but I had never told the children. I told them when our daughter came home pregnant at the age of 19. I didn't want her to marry unless she really loved the boy. I was prepared to care for the child and I told her so. (They later married and have two children.) The kids were overwhelmed. My being a birthmother became a status symbol among their friends. Of course they talked about it. If I had had any hang-ups about secrecy at that point, I had to get over them fast. Before they knew, they would come home from school and talk about a friend who gave up a child for adoption and say, "Isn't that awful." I would say it was terrible and I didn't know how they could do it, and I meant it. I couldn't even give my cat away without knowing where it was going. When I gave it away I called all the time to find out how it was doing. I didn't know what I was doing when I gave up my baby.

Later children, particularly if they are teen-agers, also pose a problem for the birthmother who has revealed her secret. What sort of message is she giving them about their developing sexuality and what she considers to be appropriate behavior for them? Her feelings are often mixed, and she must acknowledge her possible embarrassment and her concern for the teen-ager's attitude and conduct.

Young children pose less of a dilemma for the birthmother who shares her secret, because they generally regard her past experience with innocent eyes. They do not automatically share the prejudices of their society. Ideally, these children should grow up, as most adopted children do, knowing about their mother's past.

> When I told my children the older boy was nine and the younger was six. They reacted in a fashion typical for their personalities. The older asked profound questions aroused by his burgeoning intellect. The younger laid down on the floor and cried, wondering why his unknown brother couldn't come to play baseball "once in a while."

> Recently, while visiting with my birthmother, I told my two children about their birthsister. They know that adoption is not a matter of rejection by the birthparent because of my closeness to my birthmother. My son, 10, asked, "Why didn't you tell me before?" My daughter, 7, wanted to see her sister as soon as possible. Their attitude was very positive and, for the first time, we have felt very close to each other. I think they appreciated the fact that I thought enough of them as people to bring them out of the shell and into the light of truth.

The birthmother needs to be with women like her who can encourage her and help her to be increasingly open and honest about her experiences and feelings. And as she meets other birthmothers who have surrendered children for adoption and finds that they are productive, active, and interested women, she is able to develop a more positive view of herself and begin to feel optimistic that she, too, will accommodate herself to her grief. As the birthmother grows more accepting of herself, she begins to be able to conquer her anger and to understand better her family's attitudes. Even though society does not recognize the grief of the birthmother, her own acknowledgment of it allows her to be more open and tolerant. She no longer needs to see everything from the perspective of her own pain.

> Since I have been coming to CUB and started talking about it, my family says, "Well, it was your choice." My mother even said recently, "I don't know how you could have done such a

thing. I could never have given up one of my children." I think she was able to share her own hurt at last. I'm beginning to see the pressure that was put on her by my father, because I had younger sisters and because my boyfriend's family only wanted to be done with the whole thing as fast as possible.

I think that our parents had the same problem we had. They have to find out that if you open up and talk to people about things, then it won't be so awful.

When the birthmother can make the sort of statement quoted below, she is well on her way to a resolution of her grief and to the successful incorporation of her past into her present and future.

My mother said, "We kept it a secret all these years. There is no reason to talk about it now. . . . You'll never see that child." I said, "Yes, I will." It all started when I got my ring with a birthstone for each of my children. This child's birthstone is on the ring. It was my husband's idea to put that stone in the ring. My parents were very upset. "What will we tell people?" I said, "Tell them anything you want. I am not keeping it a secret anymore."

ACCOMMODATION: INTEGRATING THE PAST INTO THE PRESENT AND FEELING GOOD ABOUT ONESELF

To complete her accommodation to her lingering sorrow and develop a better self-image, the birthmother must build a coherent bridge between her past and her present. If her rage, bitterness, and guilt are to be resolved, she needs to examine honestly and without accusation, of herself or others, just what her circumstances were at the time she surrendered her child for adoption.

I was 17. Now, as I look back, what could I have done. I appreciate now that you are not yourself when you are pregnant. Everyone was so against us and we were scared. They kept telling us we couldn't manage. We had no experience to know better. We did what we were told was best. We got married five years later. If I consider now where we were then, I think I'd probably do the same thing again. All these years we were silent. I realize now we seemed to be reluctant to try to have children. If I'm going to have another child, we have to talk about it and accept that we did the right thing for where we were in our lives.

I was 16. I can accept that I did what I had to do. I did what I was told and I'm not so hard on myself now. First, I was guilty for getting pregnant. Then I felt guilty for all the trouble I had caused my family. Then I felt guilty for giving her up. Now I'm more accepting of myself. It gets easier with time. Now I talk about it to anyone who will listen.

I think that part of surviving is learning that you have to accept that what you did at the time was the only thing you could do, and that it was probably good for the child.

Once she has accepted the fact that she need not feel like a criminal forever because she surrendered a child in circumstances over which she did not have complete mastery, the birthmother has then to examine and resolve her feelings about adoption. If she views adoption realistically, she will have to recognize that, like any other living arrangement, adoption has its complexities and that adoptive parents are real people with both good points and bad. These women have grasped the point:

Adoption can be good, too. I knew I wouldn't have an abortion and I wanted to give him up for adoption. I couldn't have lived with a child as a single parent. For me it was the suppressing afterward that was the bad part, and then not being able to find out how he was doing.

Orphan Voyage[2] meetings are a real "up." I love to go to Orphan Voyage so I can have a sense that being an adoptee can be great or it can be awful. It helps to keep in mind that problems can happen even in a family into which you were born. I have to keep my perspective so I don't blame everything on adoption or on birthmothering.

Adoptive parents get the same kind of lousy information we get. They are told to act as if the child were their own, as if they had given birth to it. They are told to forget, just as we are.

Through the meetings of such groups as CUB and Orphan Voyage, birthmothers can acquire some understanding of the concerns of adoptive parents, of the pain that infertility can mean to them, and that adoptive parents are not necessarily just like them. This realization can be distressing, but it can also be constructive by placing the adoption process in a realistic rather than fantasized context.

> One of the things that helped me survive was to find out about adoptive parents. It was really painful to find out that they were different from me and my parents, who had eight children. I realize now that I made a decision many years ago and did not know all of the ramifications, for everyone, of that decision. Now I realized that adopted children are different, too. It is different from being born into that family. I didn't realize that. A lot of us gave up a child so that it could be the same as other children and not raised by a single parent. We were avoiding the word *illegitimate* by adoption. But the children are always labelled because they are adopted. It may not necessarily be negative, but it still is different.

A further step birthmothers can take to forge a link with the past is to attempt to find out more about the child they have borne. More in the past than is true today, birthmothers sometimes were not even told the sex of the baby, or were asked to suggest names for both a girl and a boy so they would not guess. Birthmothers do, however, have a right to this information and can at least obtain their child's birth certificate. The following two women's needs were the same, but their experiences varied:

> Until I had my daughter's hospital records, I had no sense of reality at all. I found out at the meeting that I could write to the hospital and they would send me their record. At least I would know her weight and have proof that she was born.

> When I got home from the hospital I immediately sent in my $2 and got the child's birth certificate. It had the same name on it that I had given the child. For me it is a document that I can hold in my hand. That reassures me that having the baby was a reality.

Increasingly today, birthmothers seem to want to go beyond this limited and formal documentation. As part of their accommodation to their pasts, they want to know more about the initial adoption, and, most of all, they want to know about their children and how they are faring. These are quests that are fraught with hazards — agency responses are not uniformly helpful or encouraging, frustrating dead-ends are often encountered, such information as can be obtained may not be wholly pleasant. Yet, whatever the outcome, simply by this acknowledgment that the past really occurred and has a continuing reality, the birthmother can make progress in her resolution of it.

I wrote the agency a letter, and in it I said that I was trying to deal with this now and it would be helpful to see the situation through the objective eyes of the social worker I saw at the time — that I understood they were required to send me the record under the Freedom of Information Act. At first I was angrier than before when I read that "the baby was good adoption material," and that I was a mature girl for my age. On the other hand, I felt better because now I was getting the whole picture and everything was more real for me.

They made me feel dirty, as though something were wrong with me for wanting to know what had happened to my child. It was just another rejection.

Actually I heard about CUB through an adoptive parent, a friend whom I had told about my being a birthmother. She had called her agency for information and they have refused to help. If a birthmother goes back to the agency, she is told she is neurotic. If the adoptive parent goes, it turns out that it is she who is neurotic.

I have two birthchildren. I sent letters with identical questions and health updates to the agencies that handled their adoptions. My daughter's agency responded by filling me in on the background of the adoptive family, accepted my "Waiver of Confidentiality" with thanks, and forwarded my updated material to the family. If they receive further information from the family, they promised to send it to me. My son's agency turned my letter over to a judge who wrote that he was not permitted to answer any questions. My waiver and medical information would be placed in a file and taken into consideration if my son ever requests my identity. What different feelings these people gave me. I will continue to work for the day when birthparents are treated humanely with full recognition of their value.

I called the foster home where I had placed him and from which he was to be adopted after I signed the release. His foster mother told me he was still there, 12 years later. She had not been allowed to adopt him. Then I called the state agency and they gave me a runaround. I called a lawyer and we decided to sue to get him back. *Then* the state acted and now he is adopted. When I first called the foster mother, she sent me pictures. Now she writes me that he hates me and I should not contact her again.

Most birthmothers who ask adoption agencies for information do not, in fact, find out very much about their children. Nevertheless, by signing "Waivers of Confidentiality" they have left the door open in case the children or the adoptive parents should ever wish to take the initiative and search for them. Eventually, the birthmother may consider trying to locate her child herself, finally to close the circle between the past and the present. Many wonder, however, whether they are entitled to make this search. Here, adoptees can throw light on the issue and help them make the decision.

At an Orphan Voyage meeting I talked to a 16-year-old who attends meetings with his parents' consent, and who is waiting until he is 18 and Orphan Voyage will initiate the search for him. I asked him how he would feel if he knew that his birthmother was considering searching, but was waiting until he was 18. He said he would feel real good just to know that he hadn't been thrown away.

The decision to search for the child should ideally only be made after the birthmother has thoroughly examined her feelings and knows her real motivation. If, by finding the child, she is trying to undo the past, to get back the child she lost, to

become the child's "real" mother, serious problems can arise
for everyone involved.

> You never want to put your child in a situation where he or she
> has to choose. It takes a lot of will to control the feeling of
> wanting the child all for yourself.

> The problem is to educate the birthmother not to pull at the
> child in order to prove to herself and to her child that she
> wasn't so awful. This is a most human feeling.

> In a normal situation you can find a child saying, "I hate my
> mother." My daughter-in-law has told me she wishes that I
> were her mother. In the case of our birthchildren, that could
> be loaded. You can't help but be glad that you became the
> "good mother." It is a way of making you feel closer. But that
> is very destructive in the long run. The child does not need
> another mother.

Before searching for the child, the birthmother must have
reached the stage in the accommodation process at which she
has control over her feelings. She must realize that she cannot
"rescue" the child or make up for the years that were lost.
Rather, she is building something new, something that links the
child to her and her past to her future, but that is something
quite different from the traditional mother-child relationship.

> I remember how awful I felt when I finally met my daughter
> and sat across the table from this 30-year-old woman. We
> were clearly related, but I had given up a little bundle and I
> wanted the bundle back. She's a mother herself, now, and I'm
> a grandmother. We had to build a whole different kind of
> relationship. We are doing it. But I was not prepared at first.

Most birthmothers postpone a direct search for their children until they feel that the child is old enough to cope with the
situation. But, whatever the age of the child, the birthmother
must realize that the adoptive parents will probably feel
threatened and that this will have an impact on any relationship
she may attempt to develop with the child.

> There are tensions between birthmothers and adoptive
> mothers in terms of power and security. You have to antici-

pate these issues and know that this is a child you cannot nurture and mother. You also have to see that there will be ups and downs in any relationship you might establish with the adoptive parents.

When I first called my son, who is now 25, he was delighted. We met and had a good visit. When he told his adoptive parents, however, they got very upset and he couldn't handle that. He's told me that he won't see me anymore. I felt devastated and fortunately the group helped me. I tried to console myself with the thought that he had to have someone to take out his anger on but that didn't really make sense. I finally sent him a note explaining that I could understand his feelings, that I was pleased we had met, and that I was glad he was well. I gave him my address so that if he ever wants to, he can reach me. I can't put him in the middle.

The birthmother can help her child to understand that the adoptive parents may feel threatened and to find ways to reassure them that their integrity as a family is not being challenged. Her willingness and ability to do so are important steps in her achievement of a sense of competence and mastery over her own life.

When I first found out where my daughter was, I called her with a story about doing a survey about adoption. She said she was adopted and that birthmothers should not try to find their children. I had talked with other adoptees who had spoken of their intense anger with their birthmothers and so I was prepared. I also figured that, at 28, she was old enough to take a chance. So I told her the truth. She said she was elated, that she had always wondered about me. We arranged to meet. She told her adoptive mother who became angry and worried. They had had a hard time while my daughter was growing up and were just starting to get to know one another. We talked a lot about how important it was not to be in competition. I was able to reassure her and she in turn reassured her mother that I would not come between them. I was prepared for the problem and that helped.

Occasionally adoptive parents will actively help the adopted child to search for his birthmother. If the birthmother has never acknowledged her past and explored her feelings, it is she who has the bigger problem. She often needs time and a network of understanding helpers before she can deal constructively with the past.

> When she was told that her son was a child who lived in the neighborhood and played with her subsequent children, it hit her very hard. When I called her she didn't want to talk about it. She said she wished he had never found her and hung up. Later, I heard her say at an Orphan Voyage meeting that it was wonderful. She had gotten used to the idea. You have to give people time. She was a very prominent woman in the community, which can be a problem if you are not ready for people to see you in a new way. The adoptive mother had helped the son find her and invited the birthmother for lunch and showed her baby pictures and all that. She came on too strong and sometimes it is too much at once. You have to be prepared.

Reunion is, of course, the ultimate resolution of the birthmother's grief, the final link in the chain between her past and her future. It may not always be possible. It may not always be totally happy. But it is real and honest, not a fantasy or a nightmare dating to some dark past. The birthmother's ability to handle it, whether it actually takes place or not, is the final proof of her accommodation to her present and future life.

> Until 30 years later, until I knew she was fine, I could not really talk about her. Now I'll tell the milkman, if he asks. I'd print it on the front page of the local paper.

CONSIDERATIONS FOR PRACTICE

The greatest source of the birthmother's difficulty stems from the secrecy with which she lived. She did not understand the legitimacy of her attachment to this baby and her need to mourn her loss. As part of her acknowledging her grief and developing a better control over her life, she is going public. She is asking, as is her right, to at least know what happened to her child and, at the most, to know her child.

The practice of adoption and the sealed record were first challenged by the adoptees' "need to know their origins." Strengthened by this knowledge, birthmothers, too, are speaking out. The material presented in this chapter is most likely to make practitioners defensive, because in large part, the origin of the problem lies in what was, and in many places still is, considered sound agency practice. If this is your reaction, then you must stop and think of the source of your reactions. Are you responding to the needs of these women or are you being protective of agency policy and practice? How do agencies rethink and change their policies in the light of new information? You must also consider your own conditioning and attitudes. Are they framed by what may be outdated social attitudes? Consider how you would react if a woman came to you and with great effort admitted that she had surrendered a child years before. Would you be able to hear her? How would you account for her behavior? Could you accept her anger with the social worker who advised her to surrender and keep this pregnancy a secret? Could you help her see that agency practice can change just as social attitudes do?

Consider again, as in the previous chapter, where the line may be drawn between what professionals can do for birthmothers and what help birthmothers may need from other birthmothers. You may be able to help them with their current depression or malaise and relate it to the surrender, as well as with aspects of the first two phases of mourning. They clearly need other birthmothers to learn how to put the surrender in perspective, to learn how to go public, how to return to the agency and initiate efforts to learn about their child. Some women may not be able to acknowledge themselves as birthmothers until they see others who have.

Legislative action may be needed to change public policy about access to sealed records. Could you see yourself working with a mutual help group on such an issue? Would your agency initiate a public education series for women using this book as a guide? Do you need an in-service training program for staff on women and loss?

NOTES

1. Henry Grunebaum, M.D., is affiliated with the Department of Psychiatry at Harvard Medical School.
2. Orphan Voyage is an association of adoptees who are searching for their birthparents. Adoptees under 18 may join only with the explicit permission of their adoptive parents.

REFERENCES

POPE, H. (1967) "Unwed mothers and their sex partners." Journal of Marriage and the Family 555-567.
"A Report on Some of Our Membership" (1980). Milford, MA: CUB Communicator.
VAN WHY, E. (1977) Adoption Bibliography and Multi-Ethnic Sourcebook. Hartford: Open Door Society of Connecticut.

RECOMMENDED READING

LIFTON, B. J. (1979) Lost and Found: The Adoption Experience. New York: Dial Press.
SOROSKY, A., et al. (1978) The Adoption Triangle: The Effects of the Sealed Record on Adoptees, Birth Parents, and Adoptive Parents. New York: Anchor.
TRISELIOTIS, J. (1973) In Search of Origins: The Experience of Adopted People. Boston: Beacon Press.

Chapter 5

THE GRIEF OF THE BATTERED WOMAN

WHO ARE BATTERED WOMEN?

The problem of abuse is not limited to any one social class or ethnic group, but is found in all communities (Davidson, 1978). In a recent national survey, it was reported that 3.8% of couples admitted to one or more attacks on the wife during a 12-month period. This means that approximately 1.8 million wives were beaten by their husbands during the year. The FBI reports that a woman is beaten every 18 seconds. On the basis of these figures, the Massachusetts Coalition of Battered Women Service Groups (1981) estimates that 52,600 women are beaten in Massachusetts in a year. Programs for battered women in Massachusetts reported receiving, in 1980, a total of 54,624 calls from women who were being abused. Some 2,000 women in need of shelter had to be turned away for lack of resources. Because of the continued reluctance of many women to report abuse, it may be assumed that the numbers given above are well below actual occurrences.

GROUPS FOR BATTERED WOMEN

Programs for battered women are grass-roots organizations which typically maintain a 24-hour crisis telephone line, operate a shelter or some sort of safe-house network, provide support groups, and offer advocacy services for their members. They work closely with legal and welfare agencies to provide the battered woman with the full range of services she may need to maintain herself and her children in a safe environment (Davidson, 1978).

In the past the law has not looked kindly on women who appeared to "abandon" their homes. Only in recent years, and only in a limited number of states, have laws been changed to permit the eviction of the abusive husband from the home and to provide the woman with protection against further assaults. Even in these states, however, women may need secret residences in order to be safe. The first shelters in this country were established in 1970, and by 1979 their numbers had risen to 300, most established by battered women themselves. Transition House in Cambridge, Massachusetts, for example, was started by two formerly battered women who advertised their own apartment as a shelter. They were quickly overwhelmed by the numbers of women and their children who needed this service, and, with the help of women in the greater Boston area, raised funds to buy a house specifically as a safe shelter.

Most of the programs for battered women operate on a shoestring and with volunteer staff. They are sometimes sponsored by local Young Women's Christian Associations and occasionally receive support from welfare departments or private foundations. Their most reliable allies have been women's groups in their respective cities.

Although legislation is pending in the United States Congress that would create a National Clearinghouse on Domestic Violence, it is not expected to pass. Battered women's groups themselves, however, have joined together in a National Coalition against Domestic Violence, and in many states there are local associations, such as the Massachusetts Coalition of Battered Women Service Groups. The following deals with how the woman recognizes her situation as abusive and moves to develop a safer, more self-respecting life for herself (and her children).

IMPACT: HIDING FROM HERSELF AND THE WORLD

The first time the man she loves hits her or lashes out at her, a woman is sent into an emotional tailspin. She is stunned and disbelieving — this cannot be happening to her. Like an accident victim, she may be in a state of shock, confused, disoriented, and vague about the details. The shock is a protective device for her, as it is for the widow and the birthmother, helping her to absorb the event at a pace she can handle. For the battered woman, however, shock can also be dangerous if it makes her unable to react to a situation in which her very life might be at stake. Unless she leaves the relationship, or insists on a fundamental change in it, she embarks on a dangerous career as a battered woman. She wants and needs to believe that the abuse was an extraordinary event, that it will never happen again. She begins to play a game with her mate that can continue for years. Every time he assaults her, she behaves as though it were a unique occurrence. Whether or not her mate makes a conciliatory or apologetic gesture, he and the battered woman never discuss his violence, never admit that the abuse has actually occurred.

Some battered women say that they live in hope. When their mates show contrition and promise never to abuse them again, they want desperately to believe the promise. Almost certainly, however, their hopes will be shattered by further abuse. The battered woman finds herself in a vicious cycle of hope and despair, which is in itself an abusive experience.

> Now I realize that at the same time I was pulling more and more into myself, trying to protect myself from hurting if it did happen again. After a while I knew it would, and that nothing I did could stop it. However, I kept thinking that there must be something I could do that would prevent it from happening again. I was sure I must be doing something to cause his anger.

Abuse can be emotional as well as physical. Physical violence is clear-cut and easily identifiable. It can extend to every member of the family and can affect material things. It is often unrelenting.

> I was married for over 17 years. He began hitting me when I was pregnant with our first child. He beat the kids, too. He broke our son's nose. One evening he started in our bedroom. He jumped up and down on my ribs and was choking me. I was losing consciousness at times. What stopped him was the phone. My son had run out of the house and gone to the neighbor's. When the neighbor called, my husband picked up the phone and I ran out. I'm convinced that phone call saved my life.

> My husband would beat up three or four guys in a bar, then he'd come home and hit me. He took all my money. One time he did buy me a car to get to work. I had it a month. He didn't like me being able to move about freely, and so he smashed the windshield and cut up the tires. He left the car sitting in the yard.

> He didn't just slap me, he would punch me around. If I fell and tried to get up, he'd push me down again.

Emotional abuse is more subtle and is often not recognized. Yet it may leave a woman as drained and as weakened as if she had actually been beaten. The "silent treatment" is probably the most oppressive, as well as least recognized form of emotional abuse. Two or three weeks of it can leave even the strongest women desperate, while their mates remain emotionally detached. Nothing the woman can say or do can bring it to an end. The power to do so rests solely with her mate, who usually does not even tell her why he has chosen to subject her to it.

> He never told me why. I'd talk to him and he'd never answer. It went on and on. . . . I couldn't see when it would end. After a while I just wanted to die.

Belittling, either publicly or privately, is also likely to be devastating. This form of abuse is particularly vicious because it is so often presented as being "for your own good." It is a kind of contest in which the woman is always doomed to lose because she must fail in order for her mate to win. Unreasonable demands by an unreasonable husband predestine her to defeat, a defeat which is the key ingredient in a relationship based on inequality. Too often, the woman tacitly assents to being treated as if she didn't count. Emotional abuse and physical violence frequently go together.

> My husband was trying to convince me that I was crazy. He would tell me something like, "Let's go on a picnic tomorrow." I'd shop and have everything ready. Then he would tell me he had said no such thing. When I would argue I would get slapped around for challenging him. Once he made a statement in front of my son, so I had a witness. He backed off, but he got me later on for turning our son against him.

When battered women have complained, society has generally protected their mates. Until very recently a battered woman who called the police found that they merely attempted to placate her while telling her mate to "lay off." Once they had cooled him off they would leave and the abuse would start again, sometimes worse than before because of the mate's resentment over her summoning of the police. The police might even accuse her of exaggerating. Her family, too, may be no help to her. They may only ask her what she has done to deserve the abuse or observe that she has to put up with it because her husband is entitled to beat her if he wants. One woman, thinking back to her call for help to her mother, said:

> My mother told me that there was nothing to do but stay. He was my husband. She was implying that he therefore had the right to hit me. Only now, looking back, do I realize that my mother has taken abuse from my father for 35 years. He constantly puts her down and every once in a while really beats her up. If she can't act to protect herself, how can I expect her to give me any different kind of advice. It's funny — I grew up with it, and I never saw what my father was doing in its true light, until now.

When others react to the battered woman's plight by minimizing the problem and disparaging the danger she may be in, she feels even more alone and trapped. Her fears of acting in self-defense grow, as do her doubts about herself, and she begins to blame herself even more for her situation. In effect encouraged by others to hide the truth of her home life from them, she also hides it from herself, accepting all of the blame. The sort of advice that battered women sometimes receive, such as to "turn the other cheek" and "be more understanding" persuade her that it must be within her power to halt the abuse and that it must therefore be her fault that it is continuing. In the long run, the battered woman herself joins the conspiracy that protects her mate as she becomes more and more self-accusing and silent.

Typically, battered women will go to enormous lengths to conceal their circumstances. They speak of "being clumsy," of "walking into the furniture," of "bruising easily," of "being hit in the eye by a piece of my son's train set while I was helping to put it together." They will turn themselves virtually inside out to avoid having to admit that they have been abused. Even to physicians who may notice their wounds, they generally complain only about tension and inability to sleep. And, if they do muster up the courage to admit they have been beaten, physicians usually simply prescribe tranquilizers, which somewhat anesthetize their feelings and further inhibit their ability to react to their actual situations.

Battered women who go for counseling often mention initially that they have been abused, but are inclined to dwell on their deep sense of depression instead. Most counselors seem to probe the past at great length, rarely touching on the women's present lives. Thus these women can be under treatment for years without any discussion of the abuse from which they suffer, and this merely reinforces their hesitancy to reveal it.

One reason for the battered woman's persistent concealment of her situation is society's acceptance of myths with which no woman wants to be associated. Most people think that battering occurs only in families that are poor, or uneducated, or whose male head drinks excessively. Moreover, as has been pointed out, many people, even battered women themselves, seem to think that the women have somehow "earned" their treatment. In fact, however, professional men have also been known to abuse the women in their lives. These men have more resources than most with which to protect themselves, and their women are especially prone to remain silent because they do not want to cause a scandal, or embarrass their children, and, in any case, they know from experience that no one is likely to believe them if they complain of abuse.

It does not take long for the battered woman to become totally demoralized. As her self-doubt grows, her self-esteem is shattered and she can no longer function as well as she once had, even in routine matters. She unconsciously adopts the contemptuous view of herself that her mate seems to hold.

> I was heavy as a child. As a teen, I felt fat and dowdy. All the time I was married my husband pressured me to lose weight. Then I would be more "suitable" for him. I tried, but he was never satisfied. I always felt like a failure. He used to joke publicly that he hadn't married a pretty girl because they run away. I always felt grateful that such a good-looking man had chosen me. After we got divorced, I was looking through photos and I saw a familiar face. It was mine — and what a shock. I was not only pretty, but I was slim, too. I had never realized how much my husband had influenced me. I had even distorted my perception of my own person.

Although, when abused, the battered woman may feel hurt, angry, and filled with hatred for her mate, she askes herself how she can hate him when she really loves him. If he is the one who is wrong, how can she justify staying with him? She concludes that she must be the one who is wrong, she must be unlovable if he abuses her, she must have provoked him past bearing. She looks for reasons to explain his behavior and winds up finding excuses for him and accepting all the blame.

The battered woman can go on for years fruitlessly searching for the key to a former, happier state. She keeps hoping that her relationship with her mate will get back to "normal" if only she tries harder to please him. She is so convinced of her own guilt that she cannot recognize how distorted her perceptions have become and cannot see that her visions of former harmony are only illusions. The harder she tries to recapture her dream, the more she is basing her life on a fantasy. She becomes increasingly exhausted and numb and becomes her own worst enemy. Instead of trying to figure out how to solve her problem, she dissipates her energies on covering up, lying to herself, and trying to make the relationship work better.

Although the battered woman tries to disguise or deny the abuse, it affects everyone around her. Her children, for example, may retreat into the same sort of terrorized silence they see in her, or they may copy their father and become abusive too. Even small children rapidly learn that it is safer to kick their mothers than it is to defend them and risk being beaten themselves. Sometimes abused women turn on their children and take out on them their own frustration and sense of helplessness. In this case they have another reason for accusing themselves — not only are they unsatisfactory wives, they feel, but they are also bad mothers.

Surprising though it is, many battered women seem unable to recognize that the fundamental problem is not theirs but that of the men who are doing the battering. As long as they appease their mates, they are actually collaborating with them and justifying their mates' view that they deserve to be beaten. These women may remain silent because they do not want their mates to have police records or possibly to lose jobs, but they are in effect giving those mates a licence to continue abusing them.

Even when a battered woman seeks help, she often does not acknowledge the extent of the abuse to which she has been subjected. More typically, she has been driven to it by a single, possibly life-threatening incident which she speaks of as though it were a unique event, neglecting to mention that it was perhaps the 10th or 15th that year. They are not yet ready to face the truth about their lives and to take control of them. One woman who had come to a shelter denied that she was battered because, as she put it, "Just to say I am battered would change everything. There would be no going back." Another woman who had had to be hospitalized dismissed the physician's observation that she did not have to put up with that sort of abuse with the simple comment, "He is my husband." At this stage the battered woman apparently is still resigned to her fate, and about the most that external help can accomplish is to ease her immediate pain.

What prompts some battered women finally to act is the need to protect someone else. Perhaps they can no longer fool themselves into thinking that their children have failed to notice what has been going on in the home which they have tried to hold together for the children's sake. One four-year-old, whose mother had left his abusive father, returned from a neighbor's house where a schoolteacher had just slapped his wife across the living room and told her:

> Mommy, I'm not going down there again. No more hitting for me. No more of *that* for me.

If the children seem to be falling into an abusive pattern themselves, the women may finally take action.

> My four-year-old started to hit me just like his father was doing. This shocked me. I knew I had to get out if I didn't want him to be like his father.

One battered woman acted on a referral from the Society for the Prevention of Cruelty to Animals. Her husband had started beating the dog as well, and she suddenly realized that this was not the way she wanted to live. Her husband had finally gone too far.

Sometimes an offer of help at just the right moment gives the battered woman the impetus to act on her own behalf.

> "How long are you going to put up with this?" "Put up with what," I asked? But I knew, and suddenly I realized that I had to do something. If the doctor hadn't asked me that, I would probably have gone right back to work and explained away my bruises again. Instead, I agreed to talk to the nurse who

knew about programs for battered women. She told me about shelters. It was hard to say, but in fact I was afraid to go home. She called to find me a place where I could stay with all my kids.

Finally taking some action is not easy for many battered women. Some women are able to stay in their own homes while seeking the help of a program for battered women. Not all mates are willing to be evicted, however, and it is the woman who must leave, sometimes to save her life. This can be particularly difficult and painful.

He was a state policeman. He threatened to have me arrested. He sometimes would send one of the men on the force by the house to check on me. Once when I said I was unhappy about this, he grabbed me and held me by the throat against the wall. My feet were off the floor. I was desperate to get out. He said that if I would give him custody of the children, he would let me go to school and get out of the surveillance of police. I figured if I could get an education, I could support the children on my own. Now he claims I abandoned them and I can't get custody. I feel more helpless and trapped than ever before.

He came in very angry. I knew I was in for it. I had already arranged to leave but he came home early. I suggested that he take a shower, after a hard day at work, and then we would take the kids out for hamburgers. To my amazement, he agreed. While he was in the shower I stuffed what I could in a laundry bag, threw the kids in the car, and headed for the address of a shelter in the next state. When he got out of the shower and found me gone, he tore up the house.

Some women practice leaving their homes, going to stay with friends, neighbors, or relatives for a few days or weeks. They may even go to a shelter for a time and then return home. When a battered woman does leave her home, she may still refuse to admit what her life has been like. She may still cling tenaciously to the thought that there would have been no abuse if only she had been a better wife. Even while living in a shelter for battered women, she may say what a great man her mate is and reminisce about the wonderful times they have had together. Only if another woman says something like, "Then how come he choked you," will she acknowledge the fear that everyone else can see in her eyes. She may still, however, say that she would never do anything to hurt him.

RECOIL: SHE CANNOT HIDE FROM HERSELF FOREVER

It may take a very long time for the battered woman whose whole life has been invested in her relationship with her mate and her home to make any significant move away from the situation. The help that is offered her must take this into account and take different forms at different stages in the woman's progression toward perception of the real issues. The battered woman's most immediate need is for protection against further physical harm. Once in a more safe environment, she then must be helped to recognize that no one, whether husband or not, has the right to abuse and assault another person. Only when she has fully accepted this fact can she begin to confront her own feelings and acknowledge that she must give up her dream of love and ideal marriage. This dream may have been realized for only a very limited period in her relationship with the man or may never have had any reality.

As she meets her counterparts in battered women's programs, she is able to realize that her problem is not unique and that it is not the result of her having failed to find the right formula for solving it. Meeting other women who once were in her predicament and who have been able to overcome it and take charge of their own lives allows her to appreciate what they mean when they say, "We know the pain, the fear, and the loneliness, but we also know you have a right to more than you have right now."

When first introduced to other battered women, a woman usually is still totally lacking in self-confidence, convinced she has been a failure as a wife, and perhaps an incompetent mother as well. She may never have worked and may feel totally blank about how she is going to manage. She may feel that she has been left with absolutely nothing. But once she has admitted to being a battered woman, she cannot go backward. The veil she has drawn over her life has been torn beyond repair, and the feelings which she has so long directed against herself must find their proper outlet. She must at last admit both the rage she feels toward her mate and the grief she experiences in having to abandon her dream that she, at least, was going "to live happily ever after." This can be a devastating time.

> The first time I let out my anger, I found myself attacking a woman in the group. She listened. She didn't retaliate or try to hurt me. How can I explain what it felt like not to be punished for yelling at her?

> I was overcome by shame, sadness, and rage, and these feelings terrified me. They were just starting a women's center and I found a place where I could talk. I don't know what I would have done otherwise.

> I finally left my husband, but not because he beat me. I really dealt with that only two years later when I went to school and took a course on the family. I read and I cried. I didn't think I could finish the paper. I realized that for 12 years I had lived like that. I had let myself be hit, made black and blue, but I never wanted to accept that it was happening.

The battered woman has to learn not to allow her rage to turn into another weapon to use against herself — "Why did I stay? How could I have let myself put up with that for so long?" She has to learn to accept the wide range of her feelings and know that it is all right for her to have them. As she does this, she is gradually able to let go of her old romantic dreams and start to build her life on a new foundation. For the battered woman, letting go means telling herself that she will never live that way again, and meaning it.

> I realized that I just couldn't live like that again. I didn't want to see my daughters go through the same thing. I didn't know exactly what or how I was going to live. I knew just one thing — I wouldn't ever live that way again, no matter what it cost me.

ACCOMMODATION: DEVELOPING A NEW AWARENESS AND CONFIDENCE

If the battered woman is to change her life, she will have to develop a renewed confidence in herself that has been undermined by months or years of physical and emotional belittling and abuse. She needs to discover that she is indeed a capable and competent person. She must find strengths in herself that she may never have known existed. Moreover, she needs a great deal of practical information about such matters as housing, finance, work, and legal actions that are available to her. Membership in a group can be a tremendously important factor in her ultimate success.

My husband made a very good living. He never wanted me to work. Every time I considered leaving, I couldn't imagine how I would live and support the kids. I knew that if I was the one to leave, I'd have a hard time getting any support from him. He'd told me so, and that there was no way he was going to be the one to leave. I needed a lot of support then to turn my back on all of this and to see how unimportant material comfort really is.

I stayed at home and came to a group. At first I was too frightened to say a word. I just listened. For the first time, I heard someone else had been beaten black and blue. I didn't feel so alone. I heard about how women got divorced and about lawyers acting for them, and I got ideas that I could change things. It took six months more and a lot more hurt before I finally went to see that lawyer.

I was so scared to go out on that job interview that my stomach was tied up in knots and my hands shook. The people in the support group were great. They bolstered me up. One woman offered to go shopping with me, another to loan me some jewelry. They all encouraged me. When I finally went for the interview, I felt like all of them were there rooting for me. It was great — and I got the job, my first job.

A group of her peers can help the battered woman understand the legal options open to her and how she can secure appropriate legal representation. She can be advised how to secure financial help from the welfare department if she needs it. She can be assisted in finding new housing or a job.

> We met in the shelter and we decided to get apartments in the same neighborhood. Our kids were friends, and we could help each other out. One of the best things we did for each other was to be available when our husbands came to visit. I knew someone was nearby if trouble started, and it gave me courage to be firm about how I expected him to behave.

Most important of all, perhaps, the support group can help the battered woman understand that nothing she had said or done could have caused or justified the abuse. It can help her recognize that she can and must take charge of her own life, making it what she wants, that her having shared her life with another person does not make him totally responsible for her happiness. She must accept responsibility for herself, as she can see so many of her counterparts in the support group have done.

> Each time I left him, I'd go back to him. I kept telling myself he'd change. This time would be different. The truth was I was scared to be on my own and I made up all kinds of excuses. I used my kids a lot for this. I told myself I was depriving them of a fancier home, good clothing, more spending money, etc. If I left and tried to make it on my own, they'd have to settle for much less in the way of material things. So what if they had to see their mother humiliated publicly. So what if they heard their mother crying and screaming while their father belted her around. I guess maybe I never really realized how much it hurt and frightened them to see me treated like that. Even when things were relatively quiet, they were always waiting for "the next time." Then one day my oldest daughter came home from school crying because two older boys had hit her. When I told her I was going to look into it she said, "Oh, Ma, you can't even take care of yourself. How're you going to take care of me?" Then it hit me — from somewhere deep down inside me I remember someone had

once told me, "The best you can do for anyone else is the best you can do for yourself. If you can't protect yourself, you can't protect anyone else." I talked with my kids then. Really talked with them. They hadn't cared about all those fancy things I had. And what's more I realized that in a way the whole thing was a cop-out on my part. I had secretly always been scared that I couldn't make it on my own. It was the reason I'd never finished college. Once I'd finish school I'd have no excuse for not trying. But if I didn't finish school, I could always use the lack of a degree as an excuse. The fear had always been there. I remembered that even as a kid I'd been so afraid of failing that sometimes I'd never even try. Anything was better than failing. I'd never realized that never trying was the biggest failure of all. And now facing my children, it had all come home with a bang. This time I had to try. My interaction with my husband was in part my responsibility. It was my life and my responsibility. And that's when I suddenly grabbed hold of my life with both hands. If I lost, at least this time it wouldn't be by default.

Many battered women are tempted to return to their homes because they have invested so much of their lives and of themselves in their relationship with their mates. They find it too painful, despite the nightmare of abuse, to put all of that behind them forever. From other women in a support group they can learn that they are entitled to impose different standards for the resumption of any relationship. They see that they have the right to expect that their husbands are seeking help and are becoming prepared to treat them as persons to be respected, not abused.

I knew he had gone for help. I knew he had given up the old buddies, the bike that ate up all our money. He took me out now. He didn't try to restrict my going to meetings. He did this for about three months. I spoke to his counselor and the counselor thought maybe we could try to work things out. We've been together now for six months and things are good. He doesn't drink like he used to, he helps with the kids and cooking. Most important, we've learned to sit down and talk to each other when one of us is disturbed by something. He treats me like a person now.

More often, the battered woman has to let go of the past and accept that she cannot change it. If she is not to continue to live as she has in the past, she must make a final break with it.

> We have been through so many "I'm sorry" scenes, "I'll never do it again" scenes, "I'll make it up to you" scenes. But he never *did* anything — he never moved. Nothing ever changed. And one day I had to face the fact that this was it. Nothing was ever going to change on his part, and I was just not the same woman anymore.

It can be seen that the battered woman is beginning to change and to take command of her life when she no longer spends all her energies trying to placate her husband and instead makes decisions for herself. Perhaps for the first time in her relationship with her mate, she is able to announce firmly, "I can't stand living without a washer and dryer," "I must have a car," "I need some money of my own," and "I want to go back to school." These statements are not attacks on her mate, but rather are evidence that she is beginning to feel like a person in her own right, someone with an identity of her own.

The full development of a new, self-respecting, independent identity can require considerable practice by the battered woman. She may be learning about herself as a full-fledged adult for the first time. Through her association with a network of peers, she can find approval for her growth and encouragement to focus her energies on building her relationships on a different footing. The continuity she needs between her past and her future must be found in her ability to learn from her past mistakes and not just regret them.

> I started dating. I knew it was becoming an abusive situation from the little things. First his calls began to be late, then they got much later, then he wouldn't call the same day he said he'd call. Then he started to criticize my housekeeping and how I took care of my children. I remembered listening to someone else in the support group talk about similar things happening to her and how we had all agreed that it was abusive treatment. I realized, "My God, this is the same thing." Suddenly it was so clear. If I let it go on, I could get involved in an abusive situation again.

Only when the battered woman has started to build a new life for herself — when she is no longer in actual danger but instead surrounded by a supportive network — can she constructively grieve for what she has lost. Only after she has become her own person can she completely realize that what she has lost is not herself or her life but rather her dreams that were, in fact, never grounded in reality. In having to give up those dreams she has, indeed, lost a part of herself, but she still retains the potential for a better, richer, and happier life.

> People in the group told me that I had really changed. I didn't see the change in my posture and my expression. I knew my voice sounded stronger and I was surprised when I heard myself laughing. The kids told me I looked better, more relaxed. I must say it took me a while to get used to accepting a compliment."

CONSIDERATIONS FOR PRACTICE

In many ways the battered woman is the prototype of the self-effacing, frightened, compliant woman who is sustained by her sense of how things "ought to be." Even after she is out of the battering situation, it may take a long time before she can reconcile her wish for reality with the relationship as it really is. She has to learn to acknowledge her own ideas and her own needs and to develop a sense of self-respect. She may have to build a new life for herself. Because so much is at stake, she moves very cautiously. In the end her need for protection may propel her into action. The practitioner has to keep in mind that her seeking out a safe environment may not be associated with her readiness to see her relationship with her husband or lover for what it really is.

She may seek or be sent for help with a depression reflected in a general inability to manage her life, for example. As noted earlier practitioners have been criticized for not being able to relate to domestic violence. The most important consideration for practice has to be a positive response to this criticism. This would mean looking at your own attitudes toward women who might be in this situation and who are having trouble telling you about it.

What would your reaction be to a depressed client who came in with a black eye and said she bumped into a wall; and a week later she came in with a swollen lip? What would you do if she said it was nothing, things were indeed fine at home as far as how she and her husband got along. However, you could sense her fear, but you did not know of what. Would you be able to pursue this with her, in a gentle but firm manner?

One approach to identifying abuse in a family is to develop a set of questions to ask at intake or to put in a pamphlet in the waiting room. These could serve as a guide to use with your client to help her determine if she might be battered Sample questions follow:

(1) Are you worried that you will not please your husband or boyfriend?

(2) Are you kept from saying what you think or are your afraid to say what is on your mind?

(3) Are you unable to take time out for yourself without feeling guilty or frightened?

(4) Are you anxious or nervous when your partner is due home?

(5) Are you relieved when your husband or boyfriend works late?

(6) Does your husband or boyfriend slap you regularly?

(7) Do you find yourself making excuses for his behavior when he treats you badly? Are you explaining away black and blue marks on your body?

(8) Are you afraid or ashamed to talk to others about the way he treats you?

If a woman answers yes to most or all of these questions, then she may well be battered. If she denies the possibility or changes the subject, at the very least it alerts you to the potential danger. Can you think of other strategies that might work?

If a woman acknowledges that she is being beaten or states this directly when you meet her, how do you respond? Do you blame her by asking what she did to provoke it? Are you able to assess the amount of danger she is in? Are you able to respond *quickly* if there is an emergency? Are you aware of a network in your community for battered women? This network should include a 24-hour hot-line, contact with the police, and welfare, legal counsel, and some type of shelter. The active helpers in such a network should primarily be women who were battered. If such a network does not exist, would you be able to help create one? The references at the end of this chapter contain guidelines that would be helpful to you. You might also find *Mutual Help Groups: Organization and Development* useful.

REFERENCES

DAVIDSON, T. (1978) Conjugal Crime: Understanding and Changing the Wifebeating Pattern. New York: Hawthorne Books.

MARTIN, D. (1976) Battered Wives. New York: Pocket Books.

Massachusetts Coalition of Battered Women Service Groups (1981). For Shelter and Beyond: An Educational Manual for Working with Women Who Are Battered. Boston: Author.

PIZZEY, E. (1977) Scream Quietly or the Neighbors Will Hear. Short Hills, NJ: Enslow.

Chapter 6

LINKING RELATIONSHIPS AND MUTUAL HELP

NEW OUTCOMES

In the three preceding chapters it has been shown how widows, birthmothers, and battered women have dealt with the critical transitions in their lives brought about by their loss of husbands, babies, or dreams of love and happiness. For each group of women, the transition involved conscious recognition of the loss, acknowledgment that their lives had been irrevocably changed, acceptance of the need to develop a new sense of themselves, and, finally, the patient building of a new identity.

The transitional process was made much easier for the women with whom this book is concerned by the availability of relationships, through mutual help groups, with other women who had had the same experiences. Through these relationships, they were able to see more of the options that were open to them and thus to learn to cope more effectively with the changes they needed to make in themselves and in their lives.

As was noted in Chapter 2, women have generally been prone to accept society's judgment that they were themselves usually the authors of their own misfortunes. Oppressed by a sense of guilt and inadequacy, they turned their feelings inward against themselves and felt trapped, helpless, and depressed. Instead of going forward, they clung to the past, trying desperately to recapture a time, whether real or imagined, when their identities in their own eyes were intact.

The women whose stories have been cited in this book were able to break away from society's traditional assessment of their weakness and helplessness. Instead, they found it possible to develop a new self-confidence, to take pride in their growing autonomy, and to learn to respect their own feelings and needs. That they were able to do so depended in part on their access to new relationships with understanding and sympathetic peers who knew just how they felt and just what their problems involved. To have simply tried to replace the lost relationship with a new one of the same sort would have been merely exchanging a past dependency for a new one. Rather, they embarked on the sort of mutual interdependency that is possible in a nonhierarchical relationship such as can exist between peers or siblings. In this context, where the peer or the sibling may be one step ahead, learning how to cope can be easier because the learner has other people's experience to use as a guide (Hamburg and Adams, 1967). Like the child who experiments with new skills and new images of herself, these women learned new and better ways of handling the stages of the transition process from their peers and were ultimately able to integrate their experiences into a new sense of their own identities.

Loss inevitably requires change. For women, the change usually means having to give up one way of relating to the world and learning how to develop a new identity with other obligations and behavior patterns. The losses discussed in this book are but three that many women experience, but they provide a useful framework for a better understanding of the way women react to a variety of other losses. The birthmother, for example, has experienced a loss and subsequent grief because of her fertility. In contrast, consider the pain of the infertile woman who wants children. It is no less acute. This woman, too, must accommodate herself to reality and build a new sense of herself. She must face up to and accept her inability to bear children. She must recognize how this fact may have damaged her image of herself as a competent, complete woman. Although she has not violated any social taboo, she may feel that her life is completely distorted and that she is in fact defective. She must learn to disengage her sense of her own worth and adequacy from her child-bearing ability. She must adjust to the fact that if she wants to be a mother, she will have to find that pleasure in children who are not from her own seed. There are many other losses that can be considered within this framework — divorce, the death of children, chronic illness or incapacity, and so on. The reader can extrapolate from the three examples in this book to other losses women experience as they read the following summary of the stages of the transitional process.

During *impact,* the woman almost invariably denies the total change in her situation and clings to the past. At this stage, association with other women, who have been in the same situation and who have not only survived but have so conquered it that they can reach out to help others, is a potent tonic. At the least, she becomes aware that she is not unique and alone. At best, she feels there are grounds for hope that she, too, will survive intact. Her numbness and denial begin to recede as she finds successful survivors with whom she can identify. Although she may not yet be ready for her new identity, she sees that there are indeed alternatives to obsession with the past.

As their feelings begin to awaken during the second phase of transition, *recoil,* women begin openly to acknowledge and accept them. Again, this necessary recognition is facilitated when they encounter other women who can assure them that these feelings are natural and legitimate. Once they realize that their feelings are appropriate and not pathological symptoms to be feared or deprecated, women can view them more realistically and begin to learn, from others who have been there before them, how to deal with them more constructively. No longer denying or repressing their anguish, they can acknowledge the traumatic events in their lives which have brought them to their current situations in a milieu, not of their former isolation, but of concerned and caring peers. In such a milieu, they can learn not only the new skills needed if they are to build appropriate new lives for themselves but also, more important, how to overcome their past socialization and learn to value themselves as independent individuals.

Accommodation becomes possible when the woman can accept and value herself for what she is here and now. It requires that the woman practice and apply her new awareness and new skills in the development of a new identity. Links must be forged between the past, the present, and the future. The woman no longer sees herself in light of her loss as someone with no role to play. Her confidence in her ability to control her own life grows to the extent that she sometimes can hardly recognize herself as the same person she once was.

A woman's ability to assert control over her life, however, requires that she accept and integrate her past, not forget it or attempt to idealize it. A woman should not be expected to forget the past or to act as though it had never occurred. Rather, if growth is to take place, and the "nightmares" of the past to be exorcised, the woman needs to recognize that it has had a permanent impact on her life but not destroyed her as a person. Naturally, this sort of accommodation will be different for widows, birthmothers, battered women, and, indeed, for women who have suffered other bitter losses, for each group is grieving for the loss of different relationships. Nevertheless, for all women who suffer a painful loss, acknowledgment of the past is a prerequisite to the construction of a productive future.

Women, then, must accept and honor their pasts, but not live in them or attempt the impossible task of trying to recreate them. Widows, for example, can instead create memorials to their husbands, perhaps take on aspects of their husbands' activities, or continue some of the conventions of their lives with their husbands as a way of honoring their memories.

Birthmothers have a more difficult problem, in that the secrecy and shame that have surrounded the experience have denied them virtually all public expression of their grief and pain. Nevertheless, they can achieve some degree of continuity by admitting their pasts — to themselves if not necessarily to the world at large — and accepting their grief for what it is, the loss of love, of a child to nurture, of the mothering of that particular baby. A growing number of birthmothers feel the need to go even further and attempt to find out what has happened to the infants they surrendered. As has been noted earlier, however, they must recognize, if they are to accept themselves and their pasts, they can never be the "real mothers," even if they meet their children, but must develop a different kind of relationship with them.

Battered women, at least as much as birthmothers, generally find the past so painful that they wish to expunge it entirely from their minds. This takes an enormous amount of energy and also reveals that the past is still so threatening to them that they cannot accept its reality. The battered woman has not buried her husband but her hopes and dreams, and her pain is aggravated by the fact that she often must have a continuing relationship with him because of their children. For the battered woman, continuity between past and future can be achieved when she is able to meet her former abuser with a new and confident sense of her own worth, recognizing him for what he is and no longer apologizing for what she is.

Finally, the women with whom this book is concerned have discovered that their identities exist independently of the relationships they have lost. In the process, they have also learned how to form relationships that include both give and take and respect for their competence and individuality. The help that is offered them as they traverse this phase in the transitional process should perhaps place at least as much emphasis on the development of relationships, which do not require that the women submerge their identities in others, as it does on their achievement of autonomy.

Women who have reached an accommodation with their pasts, or who are well on the way toward it, are able to reach out and help others who are still in earlier phases of transition. In doing so, they further enhance their own confidence and sense of the legitimacy of their own experiences. When they find that they can ease even one woman's suffering, they see in this a justification for the pain they have themselves endured. To an extent it reconciles them to their own pasts and helps them to accept their own experiences. Thus a new generation of "helpers" is constantly being generated. These women have been and can continue to be advocates for the social changes that are needed to destigmatize their situations as well as for the other services that their counterparts need.

MUTUAL HELP

A good deal of emphasis has been placed in this book on the importance to women of relationships with others and on the grieving woman's need to replace the lost relationship with new ones. It has also been emphasized that the development of relationships with other women who have had the same experience is of special value. Why should this be?

For most women, until fairly recently, their very identities have been defined in terms of their relationships with others as wife, as mother, as sweetheart. As long as there was no rupture in those relationships, they felt little pressure to see that many options for different relationships and different roles were available to them. Once those defining relationships are gone, however, they must learn new skills to assume unfamiliar roles. They can best learn it from women who can serve as authentic role models. Bandura (1977) pointed out that learning new skills is facilitated when the teachers are peers. These women may not be peers in any other sense than that they share a common loss. But from such women, they can learn much of the practical information they need in order to function in their new roles and to reorganize their lives satisfactorily. This is the heart of the mutual help experience (Silverman, 1978, 1980).

In the mutual help exchange, women gain a new perspective on their experiences, acquire needed information, and learn new techniques for coping with their altered lives. The helpers are experienced members who make their expertise acquired from experience available to newcomers and serve as their role models (Silverman, 1980). Participation in a mutual help group may be the ideal assistance during a time of transition, because the group offers women who are grieving the sort of help they need in a context which is especially appropriate.

When women feel that their identities have been damaged beyond repair, having to become a client or a patient of a professional can simply reinforce their sense of inadequacy and defectiveness. In yet another setting, they discover, they are weak, helpless, and not in full control of their own lives. In the mutual help group, on the other hand, they can see women who once were in the same situation but who can assure them that their feelings are perfectly reasonable and that they, too, given time and effort, can achieve the same competence and accommodation. They are not alone, they are not helpless dependents, they are rather women with legitimate feelings and hopeful prospects for the future.

Often mutual help groups, such as those mentioned in the chapters on widows, birthmothers, and battered women, have developed because professional agencies have not met fully the needs of some of their clients (Silverman, 1978). In other instances, they have been fostered by perceptive professionals who recognized how they can complement and augment the services offered within the formal agency setting (Silverman et al., 1974; Stephans, 1973; Low, 1950).

To emphasize the value of mutual help groups is not to denigrate the importance of the work of human service agencies, but rather to recognize that each has varying and important contributions to make. It must be acknowledged that professional agencies have not always provided the most appropriate services to all of their clients. Inevitably, agencies are products of their societies and, to a certain extent at least, reflect whatever values and prejudices their communities espouse. Equally, they have sometimes led the way to constructive change in those values. Agencies, for example, were in the vanguard of the movement to remove the stigma of illegitimacy from the child born out of wedlock and to attempt to ensure that child's future by successful adoption. At the same time, as has been seen in Chapter 4, they failed to understand and to deal adequately with the very real and painful problems of the birthmother.

Increasingly in recent years, people have themselves taken the initiative to fill gaps they perceive in the assistance they can obtain from professional agencies, and groups concerned with all sorts of problems have proliferated throughout the country. Their efforts have provided much new information on the problems people encounter, and how they can be helped to cope with them. Their efforts also have been the source of new initiatives to develop more appropriate and effective helping modalities. It is hoped that this book will help professional practitioners achieve a better understanding of their clients, the more subtle content of some of their clients' problems, and the important role the mutual help experience can play in the resolution of those problems. If it is convincing in demonstrating how professionals can deploy their resources more effectively by collaborating with their clients rather than by merely working on their behalf, it will have served its purpose.

CONSIDERATIONS FOR PRACTICE

To effectively accommodate to her loss a woman must bridge the gap between the past and the future. One way of bridging this gap is through relationships with people who represent aspects of both worlds. A relationship with a woman who has had a successful experience accommodating to a similar loss can be the link. It is also essential to reconsider the concepts of dependency and autonomy as it applies here. In these linking relationships, participants do not develop new dependencies, but interdependencies based on mutual respect and mutuality. Understanding the special value of mutual help relationships has been one of the main themes of this book. Throughout the book the point has been made that beyond any help you as a professional can offer to clients, it may be essential to offer them the opportunity to meet other women with a similar experience.

In considering appropriate services for bereaved women, it is necessary to examine carefully what their needs are. If they need to learn new roles, then you must ask how will they learn these roles. What opportunities are available for them where they can develop the skills they may need to live, for example, as a widow. If part of their learning may be facilitated in linking relationships, then you have to be prepared to make these relationships available to your clients. You can do this by referring them to existing groups that are available in your community; or you can help form an organization if none exists. Groups may not always be appropriate. There are times when you can achieve similar results by introducing individual clients to each other. Would this violate agency policy or jeopardize client's privacy? What procedures would you have to develop to get permissions from respective clients? Is there a way for staff to identify each other's clients who may share a common problem?

To organize a mutual help organization, in which the organization is run by the membership and in which they provide all the service, takes time and a special orientation. Before you undertake such a project, think through your own ideas about untrained people, using their life experience, becoming helpers? If you are not comfortable with this idea, this work may be left to other colleagues. *Mutual Help Groups: Organization and Development* (Silverman, 1980) provides a step-by-step guide for launching such an initiative.

You may want to consider organizing a mutual help support group in your agency. This is not a therapy group. You are not a therapist, but a facilitator, there to facilitate people learning from each other how to cope. In such a group would it be useful to attempt to group all bereaved women together, regardless of the cause?

Does not each group have to first deal with their own issues before they can look beyond themselves to other people's problems? The issue may be one of numbers. If a limited population is available in any one category, you may try grouping people. If the effort fails, it may be because they are not yet ready to deal with the other losses. Are there common issues that may interest all women? Some that come to mind are: employment problems, assertiveness training, and the way women are socialized in this society. When would you bring people together for groups on these more general topics? How can you use these occasions to help people share their common humanity?

REFERENCES

ANDERSON, R. (1974) "Notes of a survivor," in S. B. Troop and W. A. Greene (eds.) The Patient, Death and the Family. New York: Scribner's.

BANDURA, A. (1977) Social Learning Theory. Englewood Cliffs, NJ: Prentice-Hall.

HAMBURG, D. and J. E. ADAMS (1967) "A perspective on coping: Seeking and utilizing information in major transitions." Archives of General Psychiatry 7: 227-284.

LIFTON, R. J. (1974) "Symbolic immortality," in S. B. Troup and W. A. Greene (eds.) The Patient, Death, and the Family. New York: Scribner.

LOW, A. (1950) Mental Health Through Will Training. Boston: Christopher Publishing House.

PINCUS, L. (1975) Death in the Family. New York: Pantheon.

SILVERMAN, P. R. (1980) Mutual Help Groups: Organization and Development. Beverly Hills, CA: Sage.

——— (1978) Mutual Help Groups: A Guide for Mental Health Workers. Washington, DC: Department of Health and Human Services.

———, D. MacKENZIE, M. PETTIPAS, and E. W. WILSON [eds.] (1974) Helping Each Other in Widowhood. New York: Health Sciences.

SILVERMAN, S. M. and P. R. SILVERMAN (1979) "Parent-child communication in widowed families." American Journal of Psychotherapy 33: 428-441.

STEPHANS, S. (1973) When Death Comes Home. New York: Morehouse-Barlow.

About the Author

PHYLLIS R. SILVERMAN is on the faculty of the Social Work and Health Program of the Institute of Health Professions of Massachusetts General Hospital. She also holds an appointment in the Department of Psychiatry at Harvard Medical School, where she developed the concept of widow-to-widow programs and directed the research project that demonstrated its effectiveness. She has served as consultant to several task forces on bereavement and primary prevention, convened by the National Institute of Mental Health; has consulted with agencies across the country on issues of bereavement, mutual help, and prevention; and has worked in community agencies both as a case worker and as a researcher. In addition to her social work degree from Smith College School of Social Work, she holds an M.S. in Hygiene from Harvard School of Public Health and a Ph.D. from the Florence Heller School for Advanced Studies in Social Welfare at Brandeis University. Her publications include *Helping Each Other in Widowhood, If You Will Lift the Load I Will Lift It Too, Mutual Help Groups: A Guide for Mental Health Professionals*, and *Mutual Help Groups: Organization and Development*.

8233
'177